THEOLOGY IN A NEW KEY

THEOLOGY IN A NEW KEY

Responding to Liberation Themes

ROBERT McAFEE BROWN

THE WESTMINSTER PRESS

PHILADELPHIA

Book Design by Dorothy Alden Smith

Published by The Westminster Press ®
Philadelphia, Pennsylvania

PRINTED IN THE UNITED STATES OF AMERICA

9 8 7 6 5

Library of Congress Cataloging in Publication Data

Brown, Robert McAfee, 1920–
Theology in a new key.

Bibliography: p.
Includes index.
1. Christianity and justice. 2. Mission of the church. 3. Liberation theology. I. Title.
BR115.J8B76   261.8   78–6494
ISBN 0–664–24204–9

It is no use trying to merely modify present forms. The whole great form of our era will have to go. And nothing will really send it down but the new shoots of life springing up and slowly bursting the foundations. And one can do nothing but fight tooth and nail to defend the new shoots of life from being crushed out, and let them grow.

—D. H. Lawrence, of all people, in Roberts and Moore (eds.), Phoenix II, Uncollected Writings of D. H. Lawrence, *p. 364*

Contents

Chapter 3

THE MELODIC STRIDENCY OF SCRIPTURE:
MARX, LUKE, AND JOHN
*(From a Hermeneutic of Suspicion
to a Hermeneutic of Engagement)*   75

Chapter 4

CHORDS OF DISCORD:
A TWELVE-TONE SCALE OF SORTS
*(A Critique of Critiques: Pros and Cons,
Sharps and Flats)*   101

Foreword

The themes treated here have been increasingly forced upon me for the past five years. I say "forced" deliberately, for I probably would not have pursued them voluntarily. They have taken me into threatening territory that on any human terms I would have been glad to avoid. But I am grateful for the external constraints; I am now beginning to see the world and the gospel in ways that, however threatening, are surely more accurate than the ways in which I used to see them.

My concern is to take seriously, as a North American theologian, the kind of theology now being done elsewhere, particularly in South America, that is called "liberation theology," though the currents are diverse enough that the plural, "liberation theologies," would probably be more accurate. I feel that it is an act of North American (and bourgeois) condescension to dismiss liberation theology as no more than the latest fad, and that it is an act of arrogance to assume that it has nothing to teach us. At the same time, I am sensitive to the fears of Third World Christians that we North Americans will co-opt their message, reduce it to something we can handle (and manipulate), and thus destroy its potency for radical change—theological, political, economic. I do not think that there are any issues on the theological or human scene more important than the ones liberation theologians are raising, so in this book I am trying to explore how we can respond, without condescension, arrogance, or co-optation. The achievement will fall short of the intention, but that is the intention.

The lectures out of which this book grew began on the day after

Easter. The Easter message is the liberation message *par excellence* —liberation from the powers of sin and death, liberation for new life and new beginnings. It is the good news, the gospel. I affirm it. I also affirm that even after Easter, sin and death remain. They are part of our experience. They are even more a part of the experience of the 80 percent of the human family who have to make do with the 20 percent of the world's resources the rest of us condescend to let them have. We live in a world where political, economic, social, military, and even ecclesiastical structures seem hell-bent (the word is again deliberately chosen) on denying any victory over sin and death. We can kill everyone in the world fourteen times; that is sin and death writ large.

So while Easter is the celebration of a triumph, it is not an invitation to relax, but a call to struggle; whatever or whoever is denying or obstructing the gospel message of liberation must be considered an adversary. To believe that Christ has redeemed the situation of *every* human life means that whenever *any* human life is threatened, we are called to bring down whatever principalities, powers, forces, or structures are responsible.

As I was finishing the manuscript, I received word that my godson, Timothy Rouner, had been killed in a mountain-climbing accident in Alaska. The next day I received word that a friend in California had died of a stroke, and as I write this Foreword I have just participated in a memorial service for him. These two events remind me that there is more to the gospel than the themes of this book, which is not dealing with liberation from death or the fear of death, or many other themes of which the Scriptures speak. The book has a limited agenda, centering on the way our social, political, and economic structures not only exploit oppressed people but keep them oppressed, and it asks how the gospel offers liberation under such circumstances. Fewer people would die if we had a more just and humane economic system. But the most just and humane economic system conceivable will not keep people from falling off mountains, or deter the arrival of a stroke that paralyzes the brain. Other dimensions of the gospel offer help in coping with such anomalies. But they are explored in other books than this one.

Some readers may feel that this book is too gloomy in its assessment of the human situation, and that it is insufficiently appreciative of the benefits given to one who is a citizen of the United States and lives within the political-economic system at the heart of "the American way of life." I do not intend to promote gloom or to knock joy, nor do I relish criticizing my country. I have had many moments of joy and fulfillment and when they come I try to remember to thank God for them. Similarly, I have received many benefits from living in a country that guarantees me an unusual number of freedoms, including the freedom to judge the way my country *is* on the basis of the way it *ought to be*. But I also realize that the joys and fulfillments I have had, and the freedom my country has given to me, are unavailable to the vast majority of the human family. The rude reality is that my joys and fulfillments are frequently purchased at the cost of misery and denial to others, and freedoms my country extends to me are freedoms it denies to small minorities at home and vast majorities abroad. Having listened to the voices of those minorities at home and those majorities abroad, I can no longer pretend that it is not so.

People who write (and read) books like this one usually have it pretty well made; we are not only reasonably sure where our next meal is coming from, we are even familiar with the terms of our retirement benefits. But we are a minority. Our pleasant personal stories are not typical. We need to see and hear our stories in the light of some other stories, and in this book we shall attempt to do so. There are many other stories of oppressed peoples—blacks, women, Asiatics, Africans, Native Americans. We must listen to them all. But in a single book we cannot possibly listen to them all. And so I have made an arbitrary decision that in these pages we will listen primarily to voices coming from Latin America.

To some this is a cop-out: why go all the way to Latin America, when there are so many oppressed voices in North America calling out to be heard, particularly the voices of blacks and women? This is a fair question to which I offer the following responses:

1. It would be presumptuous for a *white* male North American theologian to try to speak for blacks. They have their own spokesper-

sons who are powerfully articulating their concerns, and whose works are widely available.

2. It would be presumptuous for a white *male* North American theologian to try to speak for women. They too have spokespersons who are gaining a wide hearing and producing a literature of a magnitude similar to that of blacks.

3. By the same line of argument, is it not presumptuous for a white male *North American* theologian to try to speak for Latin Americans? On one level, of course, the answer is "yes." It is always presumptuous to speak "for" others. But that is not (I hope) what is happening in these pages. I am only concerned that Latin Americans get a hearing in North America *on their own terms,* just as blacks and women already get a hearing in North America on their own terms. We are not yet familiar enough with the thinking and doing of our sisters and brothers in Latin America. The geographical choice could have been Asia or black Africa, and we may expect increasing literature from those areas, since liberation theologies are developing wherever there is oppression, and we need to be forced to hear them all. While their specific struggles may be very different, they have enough in common so that to respond to one set of voices should open us with greater sensitivity to cries coming from yet other lips. It is my hope that *all* those with agendas of liberation concerns—whether blacks, women, Africans, Asians, white males, or whoever—will find it helpful to hear how another agenda is being articulated, so that they can be more strongly fortified for their own struggles.

4. There is a final reason why we need to hear voices from Latin America: the problems they raise are not, as we would like to believe, far away, but distressingly near, because in many instances *we cause them.* We exploit many Latin-American countries, economically, politically, militarily; we share complicity when political regimes we support are torturing prisoners; we share complicity when our economic interests set a wage scale so low that the children of wage-earners starve. We are not "escaping" our own situation when we listen to Latin-American voices. We may be confronting the true reality of our own situation for the first time.

Such a perspective may already sound strange. Let me with telegraphic brevity indicate some discoveries that have pushed me in these directions, and why I now believe we have to listen to the oppressed in ways we never have before:

> What my nation did in Vietnam was not an exception to U.S. foreign policy, but an example of it. We do the same destructive things (more subtly) in many other countries. An experience of massive disillusionment . . .
>
> The structures of our democratic society that benefit me here at home (the vote, the capitalist system, the police) often destroy others both at home and abroad. An experience of radical challenge . . .
>
> For such reasons, much of what I previously took for granted must be put up for grabs. An experience of genuine threat . . .
>
> The place where such shattering discoveries can begin to be confronted is within a remnant of the church, since nothing less than a global perspective will suffice. An experience of modest hope . . .

The presentation of the Annie Kinkaid Warfield Lectures at Princeton Theological Seminary in April 1977 furnished an occasion to order my thinking on some of these matters, and I am grateful to President James I. McCord and the faculty of the Seminary, both for the initial invitation and the week spent in their midst. Some verbal venial sins (forgivable in the atmosphere of Miller Chapel) consequently escaped transformation into printed mortal sins (for which forgiveness elsewhere is more difficult), though I acknowledge that such an image could, if anything could, make Benjamin Warfield, the doughty Calvinist endower of the lectures, turn over in his grave.

Portions of the material were also presented in the Gates Lectures at Grinnell College, Grinnell, Iowa; the Heck Lectures at United Theological Seminary, Dayton, Ohio; my inaugural lecture as Professor of Ecumenics and World Christianity at Union Theological Seminary; and at a variety of ministerial and lay conferences. For challenges, rebuffs, and encouragement at all of these places I am deeply grateful.

I also want to express a debt of gratitude many others feel, and may not have similar occasion to record, to Philip Scharper, Miguel d'Escoto, and John Eagleson, whose vision (backed by Maryknoll dollars) created Orbis Books, the publishing house that more than any other has made Third World theology available in English. I am grateful to my students over the past five years who, in as diverse places as Stanford University, Pacific School of Religion, and Union Theological Seminary (it has been a peripatetic time), responded to the initial gropings that culminated in these lectures. And I am grateful to all who conspired to hold a "Theology in the Americas" conference in Detroit in August 1975, especially to Fr. Sergio Torres, who was the catalyst of the entire venture. On that occasion I met many of the Latin-American theologians whose works are cited below, and discovered at first hand how truly their faith is lived and not just written about. An ongoing friendship with one of them, Fr. Gustavo Gutiérrez, has been the most important single influence on me, as my frequent drawing on his writings will attest.

I am indebted to too many other people to mention names without risking important omissions, but a few must be singled out: Anne McGlinchey, for transcribing the tapes of the Warfield Lectures and unraveling many sins of syntax; Linda Clark, for patient help with the musical analogies; James Sipple, for the D. H. Lawrence quotation at the beginning of the book; Stuart McLean, for keeping me supplied with articles and essays that would otherwise have escaped my attention; Howard Clark Kee, William Wolf, Gustavo Gutiérrez, Sergio Torres, and the editors of The Westminster Press for comments on the original manuscript; Glenn Bucher, for several of his (as then) unpublished reflections on liberation themes; Joyce Stoltzfus and Livia Lopez for ongoing secretarial help; Donna and Tom Ambrogi for stimulating conversations and probing questions; Dorothee Sölle and Fulbert Steffinsky, for the gentle insistency with which they keep beckoning and encouraging me along the road to liberation; and Sydney, for the fact that her own liberation struggles are being carried out with a grace that has deepened, rather than threatened, an already spectacular marriage.

There are others I would like to thank publicly but dare not, since such acknowledgment might get them in trouble. Some of them live in places my wife and I have been fortunate enough to visit—South Africa, Peru, Chile, Argentina, Mexico, Costa Rica—and others are ones who have talked with me at ecumenical conferences overseas, frequently in muffled tones with quick glances over the shoulder. They live each day in jeopardy, because who they are, and what they say and do, is an embodiment of the gospel's mandate to live in solidarity with the oppressed. They offend upholders of the *status quo*. Many have paid heavy prices; many more will. They put to shame my feeble commitments, which may lead to occasional inconvenience but rarely to genuine hardship. While I do not believe hardship is to be sought for itself, I do believe Christians have to make choices that may entail hardship. To wrestle constantly with that possibility is both the pain and the glory of being a Christian.

ROBERT MCAFEE BROWN

Heath, Massachusetts

CHAPTER 1

Established Harmonies: A Diminished Seventh in Need of Resolution

(The Possibility of a New Direction)

> Without "songs" to God, without celebration of his
> liberating love there is no Christian life.
> —*Gustavo Gutiérrez, in Gutiérrez
> and Shaull,* Liberation and Change, *p. 94*

There has always been a close association between theology and music. A theological drama, such as Calvin's Geneva Liturgy, would be barren without the musical settings of the Psalms provided by Louis Bourgeois. A social expression of faith such as the civil rights movement of the 1960's would have been greatly diminished without the hymn "We Shall Overcome." Karl Barth's theological endeavors, culminating in twelve massive volumes of *Church Dogmatics*, would, by his own testimony, have been arid had he not begun each day listening to Mozart while he shaved. No theological statement of divine ineffability can begin to compare with the wonder and mystery communicated in Beethoven's last string quartets, particularly the Cavatina in Opus 130 and the opening fugue in Opus 131. If we wish to enter into the spirit of medieval faith, we had better not only read St. Thomas' 24-volume *Summa* but also listen to (or, better yet, sing ourselves) St. Francis' "Canticle of the Sun."

So it is not farfetched to use musical images to deal with theological themes, and we shall do so throughout this book.

ESTABLISHED HARMONIES

Musicians work within a set of rules. There are forms to be followed, conventions to be observed, limitations to be honored. To be sure, a time comes when venturesome musicians transcend the rules. "Sonata form" is cast aside, four-movement symphonies become archaic, music is written for instruments not yet designed. Beethoven's final string quartets break all the rules. Other composers have attempted a similar creative iconoclasm. Failure or success in doing so marks the distance between a shoddy craftsman and a genius.

There have also been ground rules in theology. Here, too, there are forms to be followed, methodologies that are hallowed, areas of subject matter from which one does not deviate too far, certain ways of viewing the past, and so on. Working within these ground rules has ensured that the established theological harmonies are more or less predictable; the new chords and keys do not vary too much from those which preceded them. A time may come when venturesome theologians likewise transcend the rules, positing new forms or methodologies or interpretations of the past. Failure or success in doing so marks the distance between a heretic and a genius, though one generation's heretic may turn out to be another generation's genius, and those who initially get their comeuppance may later be absorbed into the mainstream.

We can create a scenario describing shifts in recent Protestant theology, for example, that, with whatever surprises, remain comfortably within the limitation of the established harmonies. We could almost call it a metronome interpretation, since, like the bar of the metronome keeping time for the musical novice, it swings back and forth, but never so wildly as to shake loose from its moorings or to threaten the structure and intentions of the instrument itself. The shifts in melody remain within recognizable boundaries, and key changes are not bizarre.

Such a scenario, celebrated in many textbooks, would go something like this: Protestantism, as a religion based on the Bible, established its content and method in terms of certain unquestioned fundamentals. As the impact of modern science began to be felt within the church, movements arose that tried to incorporate new world views rather than stonewall against them, and liberal theology, keeping in discernible touch with what went before, sought new interpretations of old truths that would encapsulate the best and discard only outworn husks or forms. While challenging some basic assumptions of fundamentalism, notably its rigid view of Scripture, liberal theology took the content of most of that Scripture with genuine seriousness and sought to relate it to the contemporary world. When such picking and choosing among Biblical themes became a bit arbitrary (liberal theologians were a little short on "sin," for example), the deficiency was momentarily corrected by a theological successor known as neo-orthodoxy, which, while not returning to Biblicism, did embrace more enthusiastically than its predecessor many of the classical themes of the Christian past (grace, providence, eschatology, and the like), moving theologically to the right but often politically to the left, learning to read (as Karl Barth once put it) with the Bible in one hand and the morning newspaper in the other. This in turn fueled much of the theological activism of the '60s, which took for granted the Biblical concern for social justice and applied it to such explosive matters as civil rights and Vietnam. We now observe that this vast expression of energy-turned-outward is turning inward, returning to a more privatized form of contemplation, reacting against what David Tracy describes as "the romantic rebellion of the '60s," and which the magazine in which he is quoted refers to as a movement "Away from Activism and Back to Basics."[1] Full circle.

While the above is surely an oversimplified scenario (I myself would dissent from both of the latter comments), I hope it is not so oversimplified as to obscure the main point, which is that the movements described are on the whole predictable, following one another without major surprise or massive upheaval. There are established harmonies within which the melody is played. When things seem to be hanging unresolved, there is a not too surprising resolution.

A musical counterpart for this experience is found in the phrase that concludes the Gloria Patri. When we sing

world with-out . . .

we can anticipate very clearly and surely that the chord on which those words are sung, a seventh, will resolve comfortably and properly into the chord on which we sing

. . . end.

and that the phrase as a whole will bring us safely back to where we were sure we would return.

THE DIMINISHED SEVENTH

But not all chords resolve as easily back into established harmonies as the seventh we sing in the Gloria Patri.

The composer may not want to stay within the established harmonies. He or she may want to move in unexpected and unpredictable directions that may move hearers to astonishment, delight, or even anger, by the unforeseen turn of melody and harmony into an entirely different key. To produce such a transition, the composer may introduce a chord known as a *diminished* seventh, with which new things become possible. For the diminished seventh need not resolve back into the key from which it came, as the regular seventh in the Gloria Patri so predictably did. The diminished seventh can be resolved into a variety of keys, depending on which note the composer chooses to stress. Thus the chord C#, E, G, Bb

can easily be resolved into the following, and even these do not exhaust all the possibilities:

One cannot be sure ahead of time into which key the chord will be resolved; the key the composer chooses may differ from the key the hearer is anticipating. At the same time a clever composer may introduce enough preparation for change so that when the transition comes, and the composition finally goes into a new key, the astute hearer realizes, at least in retrospect, what the composer has been about, since there have been some telltale clues.

For our later theological reflection, both of the above facts are important: (1) an unexpected change is introduced, for which we may not have been prepared, which may catch us off guard, and which may suggest a basic *discontinuity* between what came before and what comes afterward; at the same time (2) that with retrospective discernment we may discover some *continuity* even within the discontinuity, and realize that we have not been flung into totally strange terrain. I do not want too easily to resolve this dialectic between continuity and discontinuity, which will concern us throughout the book, for I think we need to take the discontinuities more seriously than we usually do. But I do not want that emphasis to excuse us from examining carefully the "theology in a new key" that is emerging, on the ground that it is a new concoction totally out of touch with all that came before.

RESOLVING THE DIMINISHED SEVENTH

It is my contention that we are at a time theologically when the established harmonies are not as "established" as they once were, when it is not at all clear that the theological future will be "more of the same." We are not in the era of an *ordinary* seventh, an unresolved chord that will soon be resolved in ways we can anticipate. We are rather in the era of a *diminished* seventh, a time when a resolution is called for, but not a time when it is clear into which key the chord will be resolved.

This may be a time when different groups will simultaneously attempt to resolve the diminished seventh into many different keys, in which case we will have theological cacophony rather than resolution—a state of affairs some may feel is perennial. Or it may be a time when, one after another, different keys will be proposed and tested, only to be rejected either for not truly carrying through on the harmonies and melodies that preceded them or for not truly enough challenging them.

When we ask into what key the theology of the future will be transposed, we enter a realm in which some commitments have to be made in advance of the fact, and at the risk of being wrong. We can at least say, to begin with, that it will be a key not quite as provincial as those to which we have been accustomed. One failing of the scenario sketched earlier is that it suffers from such a fault. It was almost exclusively North American, save for a parenthetical reference to Karl Barth that could have been recast by an appropriate quotation from Reinhold Niebuhr. It said little about Europe, the World Council of Churches, the Second Vatican Council, and nothing about Asia, Africa, or Latin America, save for an implication that the United States had been fighting in Vietnam. It was devoid of references to women's consciousness or black theology. Surely the future is not with such scenarios.

I have made my own decision about the key into which I anticipate the resolution of the diminished seventh will come. It will be unexpected, harsh at first hearing to those who were expecting something else. It will be into a key in which those who have had *no* voice will for the first time be heard, in which those who have been silent can burst forth in song, in which those whose selves have been denied can affirm themselves.

Many terms have been used to describe these articulators of the theology in a new key—the "wretched of the earth," the poor, the oppressed, the marginalized, the voiceless, the exploited, the victims.

Their spokespersons vary and their agendas vary: they are women, blacks, the physically and mentally handicapped, homosexuals, Asians, Latin Americans. Some of them come from Appalachia in West Virginia, others from the altiplano in eastern Peru; some live in the barrios, others in the Bowery; some are at home in Chilean *poblaciones*, others in Malaysia. The most condescending thing possible would be to try to group them, or lump them, or generalize about them. But they have at least this in common: *they have been denied a voice and have been without hope; they now demand a voice and that gives them hope.*

Their theology is being forged in conversations rather than in academic lectures; printed on mimeographed newssheets (clandestinely distributed with no return address) rather than in volumes selling for $10.95 plus tax (though Orbis Books is making it possible for us to get some exposure to them); preached in prisons as much as in chapels; sustained by sharing bread in food kitchens rather than refectories; sung in spirituals and blues rather than Bach chorales; celebrated in borrowed clothing rather than in eucharistic vestments; growing out of experiences that gradually become the stuff of theological reflection rather than the other way around.

Our initial theological task is to take these voices seriously. We must try to understand why those who view the world from such perspectives cannot accept the world as it is; why they must opt for radical change; why they will fight for change if necessary; and why they cannot understand how those "who have it made" can remain complacent. Small wonder that they agree that the important thing is not to understand the world but to change it (even if they have never heard of Marx's eleventh thesis against Feuerbach from which this sentence is cribbed). Small wonder that they see most theology and almost all church life lined up with the *status quo* and pitted against them, by sins of omission if not commission. Small wonder that they describe themselves as "oppressed" and describe those who do not share their lot as "oppressors." Small wonder that when others tell them, "Shape up and work hard, instead of complaining," they reply, "We will, just as soon as you get your feet off our necks."

In *The Oath*, Elie Wiesel writes, "When a Jew says he is suffering, one must believe him."[2] In our world many people are suffering, many people are hurting. That is not only a problem, it is a theological problem. And when people say not only that they are hurting but that *we* are the ones who are hurting them, that is not only *a* theological problem, it is *our* theological problem, precisely because it is a human problem.

The task of a theology in a new key is to hear those cries and reflect on what we—most of whom come from a different place—are to do in response to them. For those who are hurting are our sisters and brothers.

CONTINUITY or DISCONTINUITY?

As suggested earlier, a diminished seventh can be both a vehicle for a radical change of direction and a vehicle through which one discovers in retrospect foreshadowings of which one was earlier unaware.

It is understandable that proponents of theology in a new key should stress the radical change of direction and the break with the past. For them, earlier theology has been a theology of oppressors, done largely from the vantage point of the privileged, who end up giving either implicit or explicit support to the *status quo*, or at most making modest "reformist" suggestions that threaten very few, even when the *status quo* is a bastion of injustice. There are, of course, exceptions to such generalizations, but they remain exceptions, and have not been numerous or powerful enough to justify a conclusion that the so-called "dominant theologies" will be fulcrums of change for the creation of a social order that embodies justice for all rather than privilege for a few. Consequently, the creators of the theology in a new key feel compelled to break decisively with the established harmonies of the theological past. Gustavo Gutiérrez has been particularly effective in showing why this is necessary for the integrity of the new position.[3]

Let us accept for the moment, and for the purposes of argument, that many Third World theologians are suspicious of theologies produced in situations of affluence, believing that they will inevitably be co-opted to serve an unacceptable *status quo*. Let us also acknowledge that if the rest of us are seriously to hear theology in a new key, a few continuities will also help, from which we, in our different setting, can hear what will initially sound like strident tones. This is not to suggest that everything in liberation theology will turn out to have been said elsewhere by others. It is only to suggest that *our awareness of the continuities may make us more able to confront the discontinuities.* Just as a composer may prepare the way in which the diminished seventh will be resolved, so the history of recent theology may prepare us for the new directions, so that we will neither reject them as outrageous nor be so surprised by them that we fail to take them seriously.

For the rest of this chapter, therefore, we will look at two recent theological traditions written in the key of the dominant theologies, searching for enough foreshadowings of the new key so that we can confront the latter without premature dismissal. Such an exercise, it is hoped, will give us ears attentive enough to hear, in subsequent chapters, tones we might otherwise miss. The first example, drawn from Roman Catholicism, illustrates gradual shifts over a period of eighty years of papal teaching. The second example, drawn from meetings of the World Council of Churches (Protestant and Orthodox) during the quarter century of that body's existence, cannot claim the same degree of authority as papal documents (since the World Council speaks only for itself and cannot commit its constituent bodies), but it is as close to an "ecumenical consensus" as is presently available.

Entertaining the Notion of a New Key: A Roman Catholic Journey

The first of the "social encyclicals" of the modern papacy, *Rerum Novarum,* was issued by Pope Leo XIII in 1891.[4] It does not, in many respects, yield a very promising start, although (as is the case with most papal encyclicals) if one looks hard enough, one can usually find hints of what one wants.

Leo, acknowledging that the situation of the workers is appalling, writes the encyclical in response. "Working men," he notes (and in 1891 the sexist language is appropriate), "have been given over, isolated and defenseless, to the callousness of employers and the greed of unrestrained competition" (2). A few very rich have inordinate power over all the rest. The cures of the socialists, however, are "clearly futile"; their remedies are worse than the disease. Since private ownership accords with the law of nature, socialism "must be utterly rejected" (12). Leo also rejects the notion of class struggle: "The two classes are to live in harmony with one another" (15). But this ideal harmony is interpreted paternalistically: those with money should use it wisely, giving away what they do not need—a duty of charity rather than justice. Those who do not have money should remember that "in God's sight poverty is no disgrace" (20). In fact, God calls the poor "blessed." Such reflections, Leo feels, will keep the rich from pride and will cheer the afflicted, inclining "the former to generosity, and the latter to tranquil resignation" (20). However, alongside such condescension is concern for distributive justice, a recognition that "workers must share in the benefits they create," and an admonition that the poor must not be cruelly exploited by "grasping speculators."

So the encyclical goes, back and forth, forth and back, trying on the one hand to guard against the "socialist threat," and on the other hand to admonish those who use wealth destructively or selfishly. Instead of challenging the economic system, Leo seeks to improve it by working from within.

Forty years later, in an encyclical appropriately entitled *Quadragesimo Anno* ("Forty Years"), Pope Pius XI reiterated the themes of *Rerum Novarum* in a new social situation. By the 1920's, certain Catholics had begun to question capitalism, which they saw increasing the concentration of capital in fewer and fewer hands. At the same time Europe was in the wake of the Russian Revolution, so the "menace of socialism" was stronger than ever. A worldwide depression had made attention to the themes of *Rerum Novarum* particularly appropriate.

Pius is more critical than his predecessor of "the right of private property." A "right" must be distinguished from its "use." The right of ownership is not absolute. "A man's superfluous income," for example, "is not left entirely to his own discretion" (50). And Pius is hard on capitalists who make excessive profits and provide bare subsistence to their workers (54).

There must be just distribution: "One class is forbidden to exclude the other from a share in the profit" (57). There must be concern for the condition of the workers, and criteria are introduced to determine what would be a "just wage." Social legislation to achieve such ends is legitimate, and workers are free to join labor unions to work for their common goals. If society cannot be built on class warfare, "it cannot be left to free competition alone" (88).

Throughout the encyclical, and particularly in his conclusion, Pius is critical of capitalism. There is too much wealth and "economic domination" in the hands of a few who have excessive power. "The whole economic life has become hard, cruel and relentless in a ghastly measure" (109).

Workers, Pius had said earlier, must be aware of sins peculiar to their station in life, such as the danger of succumbing to socialism or wanting all of the profits. But despite such warnings, Pius acknowledges that since 1891 *socialism has changed.* It now has two forms, communism, which must be rejected, and a more moderate position described as "mitigated socialism," which has some affinity with Christian principles. Pius does not concede much: "No one can be at the same time a sincere Catholic and a true Socialist" (120), and he is pained at Catholics who desert to socialism. But the earlier blanket denunciation of socialism has been modified.

Another advance is Pius' recognition that sin becomes collectivized in modern industrial life; injustice and fraud take place "beneath the obscurity of the common name of a corporative firm" (132), so that no one need take individual responsibility. An absolute inversion of values has taken place: "Dead matter leaves the factory ennobled and transformed, where men are corrupted and degraded" (135). This description deserves to be an epitaph.

In his brief pontificate, Pope John XXIII produced two major social encyclicals, *Mater et Magistra* (1961) and *Pacem in Terris* (1963). John inherits from his predecessors a conviction that workers have a right to a just wage, that the state can intercede against business if necessary, and that workers are entitled to strike as a last resort.

The new dimension John introduces in *Mater et Magistra* is a genuinely global perspective; the need for economic aid to underdeveloped nations to help overcome socioeconomic inequality, the use of farm surpluses on an international level, and the obligation of the well-fed to look after the undernourished without political exploitation, or, as he puts it, "imperialistic aggrandizement."

Another dimension in *Mater et Magistra* is an increasing acknowledgment of the need for "government planning," and a conviction that the state must play a more active role in ensuring the well-being of its inhabitants through such mechanisms as social security and state ownership of certain goods "pertaining to production," especially "if these carry with them power too great to be left in private hands, without injury to the community at large" (114). So the state is to be an active agent in promoting human welfare, even though socialism and communism are still not acceptable alternatives—though as E. E. Y. Hales in his book on Pope John comments, John "is embracing what many would call socialism." Little wonder that *The National Review*, edited by William F. Buckley, no friend of such trends, carried an editorial entitled "Mater Si, Magistra No"—mother, yes, teacher, no.

Pacem in Terris contains some further advances. One will be initially apparent to those who realize that during these years it was routine encyclical prose to condemn communism and socialism. It is highly significant that *Pacem in Terris* deviated from this course. If it did not espouse communism and socialism, it did not condemn them, and that (in terms of how communications operate out of Rome) was a thundering advance.

Another significant feature of the encyclical is its distinction between false philosophical *teachings* and the socioeconomic *movements* based on those teachings. Socialism might be philosophically wrong, but if it led people to concern for social justice, then cooperation with socialists might be all right, since Catholics likewise affirm concern for social justice. The message is clear: "It can happen, then, that meetings for the attainment of some practical end, which formerly were deemed inappropriate, might now or in the future be considered opportune or useful" (160).

A third significant feature of *Pacem in Terris* is that, unlike earlier encyclicals, it was not addressed exclusively to "the faithful," for example, to Roman Catholics alone, but to the "separated brethren" and to "all men of good will"—an invitation to non-Catholics to work cooperatively with Catholics on matters of social change. (John lived before sexist language had become a theological issue.)

Within the above framework, John links peace with justice, a stress Pope Paul VI later italicizes, and opts for freedom of conscience for all (not just for Catholics), a notable breakthrough that paved the way for Vatican II's significant statement on religious liberty. He includes strong strictures against colonialism and new forms of imperialism, and stresses the right of new nations in the Third World to independence from colonial powers.

Pacem in Terris appeared during Vatican II, and its influence is apparent in the longest single conciliar document, *Gaudium et Spes,* "The Church in the Modern World." Withstanding tremendous pressures, the Council fathers refused to condemn either communism or atheism, acknowledging that the church's failure to witness more clearly to its own faith had often led people to adopt rival faiths. Criticism of certain socialist and communist practices is linked with equally powerful criticism of abuses of capitalism, such as "excessive desire for profit," even though the profit motive is not condemned per se.

The Council condemned the economic trend of the times in which power was being concentrated in the hands of the few. More and more people, the fathers insisted, must be given an active share of control. The right to strike is reiterated more strongly than before, and the traditional right of private ownership begins to be balanced by attention to "the *right* inherent in various forms of *public* ownership." In addition, "It is a further right of public authority to guard against any misuse of private property which injures the common good" (171).

One section can stand as typical of emphases supported by the Council fathers. It is an extraordinary section:

Persons should regard their lawful possessions not merely as their own but also as common property in the sense that they should accrue to the benefit not only of themselves but of others.

For the rest, the right to have a share of earthly goods sufficient for oneself and one's family belongs to everyone. The Fathers and Doctors of the Church held this view, teaching that persons are obliged to come to the relief of the poor, and to do so not merely out of their superfluous goods. If a person is in extreme necessity, such a one has the right to take from the riches of others what he or she needs. Since there are so many people in this world afflicted with hunger, this sacred Council urges all, both individuals and governments, to remember the saying of the Fathers: "Feed those dying of hunger, because if you have not fed them you have killed them." According to their ability, let all individuals and governments undertake a genuine sharing of their goods. Let them use these goods especially to provide individuals and nations with the means for helping and developing themselves.[5]

What predominates in this document is the willingness "to hear the voice of God in the voice of the times," whereas the other Conciliar documents tend to hear God mainly in the voice of tradition and the teaching office of the church. Thus Hugo Assmann, one of the sternest critics of European and North American theologies, comments:

The methodology of *Gaudium et Spes,* so different from that of the other conciliar documents, becomes paradigmatic for Latin American theology. It was a first sign that the secular sciences were being taken seriously as providing data for theological reflection.[6]

To conclude our survey, we will examine two documents by Paul VI. The first of these, *Populorum Progressio,* published in 1967, sufficiently challenged the *status quo* to be described by *The Wall Street Journal* as "warmed-over Marxism."

Paul describes what is happening in the modern world: the rich are getting richer, the poor are getting poorer, and systems of modern economics are widening the gap between them. This reality is coupled with "the revolution of rising expectations": the poor have an increasing social awareness and are no longer willing to accept exploitation. Faced with such realities, Paul is more critical of private

property than any of his predecessors, and offers a stern indictment
of "liberal capitalism":

> Out of these new conditions of society the baseless theory unfortunately
> emerged which considered profit the key motive for economic progress,
> competition as the supreme law of economics, and private ownership of
> the means of production as an absolute right that has no limits and carries
> no corresponding social obligations. This unchecked liberalism led to
> dictatorship rightly denounced by Pius XI as producing "the international
> imperialism of money." One cannot condemn such abuses too strongly,
> because—let us again recall solemnly—the economy should be at the
> service of man.[7]

Paul insists that the common good may sometimes demand the
expropriation of landed estates; indeed, if things get too bad, it is
legitimate to consider resorting to violence in pursuit of justice—a
statement from which he has ever since been trying to retreat. Since
"individual initiative alone, and the mere free play of competition,
could never assure successful development" (33), the public authorities may need to lay down the objectives to be pursued by society.

In the international arena, Paul asserts that there must be direct
transfer of wealth from rich nations to poor nations. He calls for a
world tax, making strong demands on rich nations both on moral and
pragmatic grounds, reminding them that if they do not give help to
the poor, the poor will rise up against them, and insisting that when
funds are given to the needy nations this does not entitle the donors
to interfere with the internal political life of the recipients.

Finally, in a phrase that rang well at the time (though it was soon
challenged by Third World Catholics), Paul states that "development is the new name for peace," for example, programs of economic
aid to underdeveloped nations.

Since Paul is looked on by Catholics (and many others) as an
entrenched conservative when guiding the internal affairs of the
Catholic Church, it is important to acknowledge that on external
political-economic matters he is light-years ahead of most of his
constituency. Nowhere is this more apparent than in *Octogesima
Adveniens,* an "apostolic letter" to Cardinal Roy, head of the Pontifi-

cal Commission Justice and Peace, published in 1971 on the eighti-
eth anniversary of *Rerum Novarum.* Its distinction between a legal
order and a just social order has been of particular significance to
liberation theologians.

Since the letter covers the global waterfront, we shall concentrate
on a key paragraph that encapsulates the papal advances made during
our eighty-year span. We recall that Leo, in 1891, had stated that
socialism must be "utterly rejected," and that minimal concessions
began to be introduced in later documents acknowledging that some
ideas of socialists were not totally anathema. In more recent documents the word itself occurs infrequently but ideas for which the
word stands are constantly being explored. *Octogesima Adveniens,*
while papally "balanced," is more forthright than anything that has
preceded it:

> Some Christians are today attracted by socialist currents and their various
> developments. They try to recognize therein a certain number of aspira-
> tions which they carry within themselves in the name of their faith. They
> feel that they are part of that historical current and wish to play a part
> within it. Now this historical current takes on, under the same name,
> different forms according to different continents and cultures, even if it
> drew its inspiration, and still does in many cases, from ideologies incom-
> patible with faith. Careful judgment is called for. Too often Christians
> attracted by socialism tend to idealize it in terms which, apart from
> anything else, are very general: a will for justice, solidarity and equality.
> They refuse to recognize the limitations of the historical socialist move-
> ments, which remain conditioned by the ideologies from which they
> originated. Distinctions must be made to guide concrete choices between
> the various levels of expression of socialism: a generous aspiration and a
> seeking for a more just society, historical movements with a political
> organization and aim, and an ideology which claims to give a complete
> and self-sufficient picture of man. Nevertheless these distinctions must not
> lead one to consider such levels as completely separate and independent.
> The concrete link which, according to circumstances, exists between them
> must be clearly marked out. This insight will enable Christians to see the
> degree of commitment possible along these lines, while safeguarding the
> values, especially those of liberty, responsibility and openness to the
> spiritual, which guarantee the integral development of man.[8]

Socialism is no longer rejected; what is asked is "careful judgment" in relation to it. Distinctions are made between various expressions of socialism: "a generous aspiration and a seeking for a more just society" (which can scarcely be faulted), "historical movements with a political organization" (which can surely be embraced with care), and "an ideology which claims to give a complete and self-sufficient picture of man" (which would be at variance with the Christian claim). But Christians can make "concrete choices" within this spectrum and be enabled to discover "the degree of commitment possible along these lines."

The existence of such papal conclusions must be remembered when we hear liberation theologians proposing serious examination of the socialist option. Their theology in a new key will at least have had enough preparation along the way for us to hear them seriously. As Sister Marie Augusta Neal put it at the end of her own reflection on the papal documents:

> These successive stances gradually located the Catholic charism at the side of the poor of the world as an ally helping them to claim what belongs to them by right. Analyzed, these documents indicate a radical change in formal Catholic policy, from an old focus on the alleviation of the results of poverty to a new focus on the elimination of its causes.[9]

ANTICIPATIONS OF A NEW KEY: A PROTESTANT/ORTHODOX JOURNEY

Protestants and Orthodox are involved in contemporary liberation struggle along with Roman Catholics, and since the issues far transcend Catholic-Orthodox-Protestant divisions, it is fitting to look— in selective and illustrative fashion—at some of the developments taking place among the latter.

To keep control over an otherwise sprawling scene, we will focus on the World Council of Churches, an organization including most Protestant and Orthodox bodies throughout the world. The WCC (as we shall henceforth refer to it) was created in 1948, after almost forty years of ecumenical effort to reverse centuries of Christian division.[10] The WCC brought together two ecumenical streams, Faith and Order, concentrating on internal theological and ecclesiological issues, and Life and Work, stressing the relation of the church to social, economic, and political questions. It is the latter set of emphases that will chiefly concern us.[11]

There have been five world assemblies of the WCC constituencies: Amsterdam 1948, Evanston 1954, New Delhi 1961, Uppsala 1968, and Nairobi 1975. Sandwiched in between have been regional conferences and special gatherings dealing with more narrowly specified themes, to a few of which we will also refer.

In the days preceding the WCC, ecumenical Life and Work gatherings laid stress on Christian involvement in movements for social change in such areas as economics, politics, racism, education, and war. The rise of totalitarian movements in Europe in the 1930's pressed delegates to look for resources with which to stand fast against fascism and create alternate social structures. The term that emerged to characterize such discussions in the post-World War II Amsterdam and Evanston assemblies was "the responsible society." The Amsterdam Assembly offered critiques of both communism and laissez faire capitalism:

> Each has made promises which it could not redeem. Communist ideology puts the emphasis on economic justice, and promises that freedom will come automatically after the completion of the revolution. Capitalism puts the emphasis on freedom, and promises that justice will follow as a by-product of free enterprise; that, too, is an ideology that has been proven false.[12]

The alternative was defined as follows:

> A responsible society is one where freedom is the freedom of men who acknowledge responsibility to justice and public order, and where those who hold political authority or economic power are responsible for its exercise to God and the people whose welfare is affected by it. . . . It is required that people have freedom to control, to criticize and to change their governments, that power be made responsible by law and tradition, and be distributed as widely as possible through the whole community. (Pp. 77–78)

It gradually became apparent that such concerns, admirable in themselves, were almost exclusively the product of the "western" liberal democratic tradition, and one of the great virtues of the WCC has been its ability to provide a platform for other political, social, and theological traditions. This can be illustrated by the deliberations of the Lucknow conference in December 1952, in which concern for the responsible society was examined from East Asian perspectives.[13]

Starting with an acknowledgment that "A social revolution is taking place in East Asia," the delegates asked about their Christian responsibility in the face of that reality. A specific issue raised by the "social revolution" was the need for land reform, "to get rid of the old feudal land-holding relationships," but also for "the creation of social and legal conditions which will make it possible for a new and more just system of land development and community life to succeed" (p. 144). Ownership of small farms by those who work the land, low interest rates, utilization of unused land, and provision for landless peasants were among the proposals advocated.

The discussion of industrialization for East Asia stressed the need for "the social planning state," the nationalization of key industries with the maintenance of some private enterprise, while recognizing that "in the present situation of East Asia, however, it is the state which can take the initiative and encourage saving and investment by the people" (p. 146).

Dealing with the effects of the international situation on their social and economic reconstruction, the East Asians insisted that

> when American foreign policy is determined primarily by the criterion of anti-Communism it generally strengthens conservative and reactionary political groups in the East Asian scene and tends to weaken the forces of healthy social reform. (P. 147)

Prophetic words that later U.S. intervention tragically validated.

The delegates similarly scored the international arms race as reducing their own economic capacity, and the western stress on military defeat of communism as "a threat to movements of national freedom and justice" (p. 147). They gave a firm declaration of the need for national self-determination over against the colonialist tendencies of the world powers vis-à-vis East Asia, and acknowledged that "defense against Communism might become a means of suppressing the movement of national liberation and social justice," along with recognition that "national liberation movements are in danger of being exploited by world Communism and abusive tyrannies" (p. 149).

After indicating that a responsible society *in East Asia* would be a place where:

1. social justice is actively promoted,
2. full development of natural resources is pursued,
3. the fullest share possible of the national wealth is guaranteed to all,
4. human rights and freedoms are effectively guaranteed,
5. the people have full sovereignty for their own affairs,
6. the principles of social justice and political life are in accordance with the concept of a man as a person called to responsible existence in community (p. 150),

the delegates concluded that they must "accept the necessity of political action as a means of promoting social justice" (p. 151). This would sometimes mean "the creation of healthy secular political movements," or "judging and redeeming movements which are already working for social justice within a democratic framework" (p. 151). Rather than organizing Christian political parties, this would mean working with others for the basic changes for which the "social revolution" in East Asia calls.

The discussion of a responsible society was continued at the Evanston Assembly in 1954, "not as an alternative social or political system, but a criterion by which we judge all existing social orders and at the same time a standard to guide us in the specific choices we have to make."[14]

While reaffirming previous strictures against Marxist ideology and totalitarian practice, the Assembly went on to stress that "the growth of communism is a judgment upon our modern societies generally for past or present indifference to social justice, in which the Church is also involved" (p. 121). Along with recognition that there is always a "temptation to succumb to anti-communist hysteria" went recognition of the "temptation to accept the false promises of communism"

(p. 122). A new stress at Evanston was heightened recognition of "the problems in the economically underdeveloped regions" (pp. 123–126), and the importance of acknowledging "the urge to national self-determination" in such regions. In arriving at these conclusions, the delegates relied heavily on the insights of the Lucknow conference.

While the assembly at New Delhi in 1961 continued to deal with "the responsible society," the theme was already beginning to be subordinated to a new one, "Rapid Technological and Social Change," a reminder from the so-called "younger churches" that the time was one of revolution, and that Christians needed to respond creatively rather than fearfully to movements of rapid change.[15] New Delhi also initiated discussion of the need for "a world strategy of development," and a more sensitive response to the importance of increasing production and raising living standards. The danger of imposing "western" cultural assumptions on other parts of the world was particularly noted. So while the earlier criteria of a responsible society were still affirmed, they were seen to need constant reexamination in the light of the emergence of new nations, who could not be expected to jump overnight into a balanced dialectic of freedom and order.

The emerging concerns of Third World Christians came most clearly into focus at the conference of the Church and Society Commission of the WCC held in Geneva in July 1966, on the theme "Christians in the Technical and Social Revolutions of Our Time." By any accounting, this conference is a watershed in ecumenical history, and in terms of the concerns of this chapter it is the most important single event. For the first time at a large ecumenical gathering, lay delegates outnumbered clerics, and more important, Third World Christians were finally granted a major platform. They used it well. It soon became apparent that the "cold war" mentality (suggesting that the struggle was east vs. west, Russia vs. the United States, communism vs. capitalism) was being replaced by recognition that the real struggle was north vs. south, rich vs. poor, white vs. colored. The "social revolutions of our time" would be between northern rich white nations and southern poor colored nations. The former have a minority of the population but most of the wealth and power, and division of the world's resources was no longer going to be accepted with equanimity by the impoverished majority. 'Bola Ige, a Nigerian lawyer, well represented the mood of the Third World delegates:

> There can be no peace in the world where two-thirds of mankind are patronizingly referred to as "the poor," "the underdeveloped," "the third world," and now "the newly awakened peoples." There can be no peace in the world where 75 nations have their economic (and therefore their political) future dictated by the narrow self-interest of Europe and America. There can be no peace where the Soviet Union and the United States arrogate to themselves the monopoly of directing the future of the world and of other nations. And there can be no peace as long as there is any colony in the world, and as long as neo-colonialism remains more vicious than its parent—colonialism.[16]

Mr. Ige, citing the tremendous imbalances in the distribution of the world's goods, did not demand that all of it be redistributed to the Third World nations, but he did demand "that we take part in seeing that this enormous wealth and technology are not used to our detriment" (p. 18).

Instead of attempting the impossible task of "summarizing" the results of the conference, we will note sample emphases from the section reports.

On the matter of priorities of concern for the churches, the conference was clear: "Christians must insist that priority be given to the needs of the poorest sections of society, and above all to those of the developing world" (p. 60). In fleshing out the concern, the report recognized that the *rapid* economic growth necessary to lessen the gap between the rich and the poor "can be achieved only through some form of conscious planning" (p. 78). Such a contention was held to be "beyond dispute," and a decision was made to bypass the now-empty polemics of trying to force decisions between "unregulated free enterprise and completely controlled central planning," and to recognize that "a general consensus in favor of some degree of mixed economy has emerged" (p. 78). This allows for recognition that different economic approaches can be appropriate to different regions and among countries at different stages of their own growth toward economic maturity. The report urged carefully worked out "development" schemes, by which resources from the developed world could be made available to developing nations, through loans, outright gifts of money, goods or personnel, and other exchanges. The WCC was mandated to pursue (in cooperation with the Roman Catholic Church if possible) the following proposals:

a. the development of regional and world-wide institutions to coordinate national and international efforts for the promotion of economic and social justice;
b. the possibilities of the transfer of resources from armaments to development aid;
c. the possibilities of instituting a system of international taxation for world development. (P. 92)

On another level the delegates recognized that in some situations it was not possible to wait for legal changes:

> When for generations peasants have been exploited by great landowners, may Christians appeal to the established conventional laws of property? Must they not rather actively participate in radical redistribution of land? May they do so even when no provisions of institutional or statutory law provide for such basic change? Many Christians see not only that such revolutionary acts are to be condoned when done by others but also their own duty to participate actively. (P. 102)

Such reflections inevitably raised the question of the appropriateness of violence when confronting inflexible social injustice. Geneva stressed the then rather-new recognition that violence is covertly present in unjust social structures long before it appears as overt revolt against those structures:

> Violence is very much a reality in our world, both the overt use of force to oppress and the invisible violence *(violencia blanca)* perpetrated on people who by the millions have been or still are the victims of repression and unjust social systems. Therefore the question often emerges today whether the violence which sheds blood in planned revolutions may not be a lesser evil than the violence which, though bloodless, condemns whole populations to perennial despair. . . .
> It cannot be said that the only possible position for the Christian is one

of absolute non-violence. There are situations where Christians may become involved in violence. Whenever it is used, however, it must be seen as an "ultimate recourse" which is justified only in extreme situations. (Pp. 115–116)

Another report offered two generalizations about the approach of Christians to the reorganization of power structures in the Third World:

One is that wherever small *élites* rule at the expense of the welfare of the majority, political change toward achieving a more just social order as quickly as possible should be actively promoted and supported by Christians. The second is that, in cases where such changes are needed, the use by Christians of revolutionary methods—by which is meant violent overthrow of an existing political order—cannot be excluded *a priori*. For in such cases, it may very well be that the use of violent methods is the only recourse of those who wish to avoid prolongation of the vast covert violence which the existing order involves. But Christians should think of the day after the revolution, when justice must be established by clear minds and in good conscience. There is no virtue in violence itself, but only in what will come after it. (P. 143)

In responding to specific suggestions for promoting economic development, Catholics and Protestants formed a provisional Commission on Society, Development, and Peace (producing the acronym SODEPAX), which jointly sponsored an ecumenical conference at Beirut in April 1968 on the theme "World Development: Challenge to the Churches," which worked out detailed proposals for economic aid and development programs. These refinements of the Geneva concerns went to the Fourth Assembly of the WCC held at Uppsala in July 1968.

Among other achievements, Uppsala gave formal ratification to the concern expressed at both Geneva and Beirut for more extensive ecumenical cooperation. SODEPAX was accepted as an official body representing both the WCC and the Roman Catholic Church, a unity symbolized by making a Jesuit the chairman and locating the headquarters in Geneva.

In addition to widespread discussion on international affairs, refugees, displaced persons, "selective conscientious objection" to war, and racism (to which we shall return later), Uppsala had a section dealing with "World Economic and Social Development." The report of this section emphasized the need for the developed nations to "shed all tendencies to exploit economically or to dominate the poorer, and therefore weaker, economies of other nations."[17] The positive implications of such a stand were spelled out specifically by stressing the need for developed nations to take an active part in the

> creation of supra-national structures to deal with regional and world economic planning involving the stabilization of the world market; an international taxation system to provide funds for development; increase of multilateral aid programs and formulation of regional associations of countries for economic cooperation, as steps toward a wider international community. (Pp. 48–49)

All member churches were asked to contribute to development projects in addition to whatever they were already spending on missions and other programs in such proportion "as would entail sacrifice."

In addition to funding development programs of their own, the churches were urged to become politically involved in their own countries, particularly to force political parties to give a high priority to development concerns, to press each nation to reach a goal by 1971 of contributing one percent of its GNP to an international monetary pool for developing nations to draw on, to allow citizens to perform alternate volunteer service in development projects in lieu of time in the armed forces, and "to participate in a responsible way in movements for radical structural changes necessary to establish more justice in the society" (p. 53).

Uppsala's ratification of SODEPAX as an official body gave impetus to ecumenical cooperation on further programs of economic aid and development, and such projects continue at the present time. But these emphases soon began to be viewed by Third World Christians as too establishment-oriented, likely to perpetuate ongoing injustice by responding to immediate needs rather than exploring underlying causes that produce such needs. A small conference at Montreal in 1969 voiced trenchant critique of schemes that might perpetuate structures of injustice. There was a head-on confrontation with the whole structural-systemic question, and a willingness to draw some uncomfortable conclusions. The possible need for violent change as a last resort was again affirmed:

> There can be non-violent revolutions. All our efforts must be directed to change without violence. But if injustice is so embedded in the status quo and its supporters refuse to admit change, then as a last resort men's consciences may lead them in full and clearsighted responsibility without hate or rancor to engage in violent revolution. A heavy burden then rests on those who have resisted change.[18]

There was recognition that since the present distribution of economic power in the world is untenable, strong measures are called for:

> We are already clear that *most of the existing power relationships are morally unjustifiable and economically oppressive.* Further study is needed less to determine the moral status of these relationships than to emphasize effectively *the necessity of overthrowing them,* especially in areas where economic power is combined with racism and the repression of whole ethnic groups. (P. 23, italics added)

The conference concluded that "the present social and economic order is inadequate to accommodate the mounting pressures that are being generated" from the poor and the dispossessed, and indicated that there are two possible responses: the first would be to seek to contain "the mounting pressures" by the use of power to maintain the present unjust distribution of resources, whereas the second would be "for Christians to join with all men who are struggling for a more just society," insisting on maximum participation by all, rather than letting decisions be made by the few for the many.

> For Christians only the second alternative is possible. But such a course necessarily involves *radical reorganization of existing relationships between and within nations.* . . . Such reorganization is inevitably traumatic and frequently dangerous, since it is resisted by those who opt for the first alternative. . . . The work of SODEPAX is no less than to engage the churches in this process, prepare them for the trauma, call them to action, encourage them in the danger, and inspire them in the vision. (P. 25, italics added)

This is as forthright a "call for revolution" as one could conceive coming forth from a committee, and it remains a challenge to all subsequent accommodationist or reformist alternatives.

Further conferences have been held under both SODEPAX and WCC sponsorship; their reports reflect increasing recognition that "developmentalism" runs the danger of perpetuating structures of injustice by settling for cosmetic adjustment around the edges, along with anticipations that the motif of "liberation" might provide a better image for the radical transformations needed. (A symbol of this shift: at a 1969 SODEPAX consultation on "Theology and Development," Gustavo Gutiérrez gave a paper on "The Meaning of Development"—actually an outline of his later book *A Theology of Liberation*—that not only criticized development models but offered a liberation model in their stead.)

As C. I. Itty has pointed out, there have thus been gradual shifts in WCC thinking on the development question.[19] Emphasis was initially on economic development, assuming that increases in the gross national product of a country would benefit the masses. This was later challenged, since even when the GNP is increased this usually benefits only the already rich, leaving the poor in a comparatively worse position than ever. Three criteria must therefore be interrelated. *(a)* economic growth, *(b)* self-reliance on the part of developing nations, so that they escape the situation of dependency, and *(c)* social justice, so that the gains are fairly shared by all. This means a new emphasis upon the "criterion of the human," recognizing that persons want freedom and dignity as well as food, which in turn means a new emphasis on the need for *structural* change.

So an initial stress on "the responsible society" with its largely "western" bias, having been gradually replaced by theology of development and a concern for the dispossessed, is itself being transformed in the direction of liberation concerns. As Itty puts it:

> It was recognized that revolutionary changes in sociopolitical structures can come about only by a process of liberation involving the masses. Conscientization, organization and capacitation of the people were therefore recognized as vital elements in the liberation struggle. (P. 17)

This is not to suggest that the WCC has emerged as the institutional champion of "liberation theology." But it is to suggest that its own history has surfaced the importance of liberation themes, and we will cite two further conferences as examples of such awareness.[20]

A conference on "Salvation Today," held in Bangkok in January 1973 under the auspices of the Commission on World Mission and Evangelism of the WCC, not only acknowledged the individual dimension of salvation but insisted on stressing the social dimension as well—a fact that greatly disturbed some of the delegates. But as Emilio Castro, formerly President of the Evangelical Methodist Church of Uruguay and now on the WCC staff, reported:

> We found that . . . Christian participation in struggles for social justice, especially in actions favouring the powerless of the world, is not a deviation from the main concern of the Christian faith but precisely the relevant manifestation of it in today's world.[21]

Comments from the section of the conference on "Salvation and Social Justice" illustrate Dr. Castro's appraisal:

> As evil works both in personal life and in exploitative social structures which humiliate humankind, so God's justice manifests itself both in the justification of the sinner *and in social and political justice.* As guilt is both individual and corporate so God's liberating power changes both persons *and structures.* (P. 199, italics added)

This has important implications for the churches:

> Without the salvation of the churches from their captivity in the interests of dominating classes, races and nations, there can be no saving church. Without liberation of the churches and Christians from their complicity with structural injustice and violence there can be no liberating church for mankind. . . . We must confess our misuse of the name of Christ by the accommodation of the churches to oppressive powers. (P. 200)

The context of such conclusions is clear: there are a number of social dimensions in a "comprehensive notion of salvation":

1. Salvation works in the struggle for economic justice against the exploitation of people by people.

2. Salvation works in the struggle for human dignity against political oppression by their fellow men.
3. Salvation works in the struggle for solidarity against the alienation of person from person.
4. Salvation works in the struggle of hope against despair in personal life. (P. 200)

The insistence that each of these dimensions must be related to the others makes clear that even a doctrine as personal as "salvation" cannot avoid the social-structural aspects of the gospel.

The most recent world assembly of the WCC was held in November-December of 1975 in Nairobi. The theme of the Assembly, "Jesus Christ Frees and Unites," lent itself naturally to the expression of liberation concerns, and much attention was given to Jesus the Liberator. There were tensions within the Assembly centering on determination not to lose stress on individual personal salvation in a morass of socioethical analysis (some of the delegates being intent to recoup what they felt were the "losses" of Bangkok), but there was no retreat at Nairobi into privatism, and the report on "Confessing Christ Today" kept the dialectic between individual conversion and radical social transformation very much alive.[22]

At another important point Nairobi opted for the oppressed. After the Uppsala Assembly, the WCC had created a Program to Combat Racism, which dispensed considerable sums of money to agencies working for racial justice. A number of grants went to "liberation groups" in black Africa, the rationale being that it was not appropriate for white liberals to make decisions about how blacks should escape from bondage, and that those seeking their own liberation were the best judges about what they needed to do. Enormous pressure was exerted on the WCC, not only by white South Africans but by a number of European churches, to clip the wings of the Program to Combat Racism, which was accused of sponsoring violence, fostering divisiveness and enhancing the spread of terrorism. The Assembly, however, overwhelmingly reaffirmed the Program and voted to increase its activities in the future.[23]

Nairobi also reiterated that structural deficiencies in the present unjust order call for radical patterns of change:

Poverty, we are learning, is caused primarily by unjust structures that leave
resources and the power to make decisions about the utilization of resources in the hands of a few within nations and among nations, and that
therefore one of the main tasks of the Church when it expresses its
solidarity with the poor is to oppose these structures at all levels. . . . This
makes it necessary to examine critically the economic and social goals, the
patterns of resource ownership and decision-making processes in the local
and national situations, as also at the international context, to reject all
patterns that oppress the poor and to work for those which release the
creative powers of people to satisfy their needs and decide their destiny.
(P. 123)

Since one of the Nairobi sections also dealt with "Structures of
Injustice and Struggles for Liberation," we can assume that recognition of the structural root of injustice is firmly anchored in ecumenical thinking, and that those who see the implications of such an
analysis will find themselves within hailing distance of the concerns
of liberation theology.

THE POSSIBILITY OF ATTENTIVENESS TO THEOLOGY IN A NEW KEY

What do these two case studies tell us? They indicate that there
has been a gradual, often reluctant, recognition that the plight of the
poor and the dispossessed deserves more central attention than it has
received in the past, and that to take such emphasis seriously means
to call into question the structure of contemporary society, which
needs more than just a little reforming. If we do not hear clarion calls
for revolution, at least we detect increasing discomfort with the way
things are.

If it is not exactly clear where Christians are to go with that, it is
at least clear that they must go somewhere *new*, and that a mere
repetition of the past will not suffice. Thus we are brought to the
diminished seventh, even if we are not yet clear what the new key
will be. Perhaps that is enough for the moment—it will at least give
us ears willing to listen to resolutions into a new key, some understanding of our world and the task of Christians within it that we

would be less likely to hear, had we not gone through the exercise.

So we turn now to hear how exponents of theology in a new key make their case. For the next two chapters we will listen as attentively as we can. Only after having done so will we have earned the right to entertain criticisms of the position (Chapter 4) before we go on to ask what it means for us (Chapters 5 and 6).

CHAPTER 2

A Challenge
to the Established Harmonies:
"The View from Below"

(Liberation as a New/Old Note)

> There remains an experience of incomparable value. We
> have for once learnt to see the great events of world
> history from below, from the perspective of the outcast,
> the suspects, the maltreated, the powerless, the op-
> pressed, the reviled—in short, from the perspective of
> those who suffer.
> —*Dietrich Bonhoeffer,* Letters and Papers
> from Prison, *enlarged edition, p. 17*

This extraordinary admission by Dietrich Bonhoeffer, commenting
to his bourgeois friends about what they have learned "After Ten
Years" in the resistance movement against Hitler, is not used to
suggest that Bonhoeffer was really "the first liberation theologian,"
but to indicate that it is sometimes possible for those who come out
of mainline Christianity to put cherished presuppositions on the line,
and begin to see things in a new way.

There was nothing in Bonhoeffer's background to suggest that he
—son of affluent parents and inheritor of an orthodox Lutheranism
—would cast his lot with what he calls "the outcast, the suspects, the
maltreated, the powerless, the oppressed, the reviled." And yet the
force of historical circumstances did initiate the remarkable shift the
above excerpt records. We do not know where Bonhoeffer's adoption
of "the view from below" would have led him, aside from a few hints

in his last letters, but it is clear that he felt himself called to risk much in response to the pressure of unanticipated demands.

The closest analogy from Latin America is Camilo Torres of Colombia, also the son of well-to-do parents, who received a comfortable upbringing, was educated abroad at Louvain, consecrated to the life of the church through ordination to the priesthood, and like Bonhoeffer, was comfortably established at a university. But Fr. Torres also found that historical circumstances forced him in unanticipated directions, so that he who was born in comfort had to throw in his lot with the poor, endure castigation by his religious superiors, and finally join the resistance as a guerrilla fighter in the Colombian jungles, meeting violent death as Bonhoeffer also did.[1]

The two lives make clear that those to whom it is initially foreign can, on occasion, adopt "the view from below," and see life from that perspective because they are attempting to *live* from that perspective. Such a shift of perspective is not unfamiliar in Christian history; it is called *conversion.*

In both instances it was the force of circumstances, or more accurately *a new perception of the plight of others,* that initiated such radical shifts in the lives of Dietrich Bonhoeffer and Camilo Torres. And as those circumstances and those perceptions were brought into range of the Christian perspective both men had inherited, it became clear that their received understanding of the faith had to undergo modification. The established harmonies of their lives were challenged in a way that meant abrupt transposition into a new key.

We saw earlier that there have been a few preparations for such transposition in recent Catholic and Protestant history. That recital should have prepared us to hear more clearly the new notes that are emerging. But the experience of Bonhoeffer and Torres should now prepare us for an acceleration of the process; there is not as much time as we would like. The cries of the poor will not accommodate themselves to our time schedules. The recorded shift in Roman Catholic teaching took eighty years. Such majestic pace is a luxury the future will not permit us.

We learn from Bonhoeffer and Torres that those in positions of privilege can be changed. Since this book is addressed primarily to such persons, the assumption must be adopted as a working principle: *we are not doomed to remain where we are.* If it is difficult for the rich to enter the Kingdom of Heaven, it is almost as difficult for the comfortable to entertain notions that challenge their comfort. But if "with God all things are possible," we can risk contemporary challenges to the familiar established harmonies. We may even be able to hear the theology in a new key sensitively enough to join the chorus, and Bonhoeffer's notion of "the view from below" provides a perspective from which we can hold together many of the strands that characterize liberation theology, which is preeminently a way of looking at life "from below," from the perspective of the poor, the dispossessed, the marginalized.

A Geographical/Historical Excursion: From Medellín 1968 to Santiago 1972

In our Roman Catholic historical excursion in Chapter 1 we noted a gradual if cautious "opening to the left," so that the socialist option, anathema in 1891, was at least entertainable by 1971. This sequence ignored two Latin-American events that are crucial to an understanding of theological developments on that continent. The first of these was the conference of Latin-American bishops (CELAM), held at Medellín, Colombia, in August 1968; the second was the movement Christians for Socialism that reached a high-water mark in a conference at Santiago, Chile, in April 1972.

The Medellín conference is the first instance in which a significant portion of the Roman Catholic hierarchy has acknowledged the structural nature of evil and has analyzed violence as a component of the unjust structures. This analysis became a springboard from which more radical analyses could be initiated with at least the presumption of hierarchical support, and Medellín has been a major catalyst in social engagement by Latin-American clergy and laity.

The theme of the conference was "The Church in the Present-Day Transformation of Latin America in the Light of the [Second Vatican] Council." What emerged from Medellín suggests a reversal of the title, for example, "The Present-Day Transformation of the

Council in the Light of Latin America," since although the Medellín documents are copiously footnoted with conciliar texts and papal encyclicals, they occasionally go far beyond what Vatican II explicitly stated. "Medellín hurts," one of the bishops commented afterward, "because it demands radical changes and abandoning of certain privileged positions." This is not to say that Medellín is consistently "radical" or that it cheats on its conciliar resources. The sixteen documents cover a wide range of perspectives, and the ones of most interest to our present study are those dealing with "Peace," "Poverty in the Church" and to a lesser degree "Justice" and "Education." We will use the text on "Peace" as indicative of new emphases.[2]

Present-day Latin-American underdevelopment is described as "an unjust situation which promotes tensions that conspire against peace" (p. 71). There are *tensions between classes* resulting from "internal colonialism," based on the marginality of many groups and the extreme inequality that results, leading to growing frustration, particularly when "rising expectations" are systematically blocked by those in power. There is not only "a lamentable insensitivity of the privileged sectors to the misery of the marginated sectors," but a calculated "use of force to repress drastically any attempt at opposition" (p. 72). Crusades against communism and on behalf of "order" are invoked by the privileged to prevent change. There are also *international tensions.* Latin-American nations live in dependency on foreign powers; there has been a shift from previous patterns of political colonialism to economic domination, now described as "external colonialism." This situation of dependency guarantees that "the countries which produce raw materials . . . always remain poor, while the industrialized countries enrich themselves" (pp. 73–74). The already existing imbalances are exacerbated by the rapid flight of economic and human capital to rich countries, the evasion of established tax systems by the foreign countries, and "the international imperialism of money" (cited from Pius XI's encyclical *Quadragesimo Anno*). A third tension exists *between Latin-American countries* in the increasing nationalism and consequent escalation of the arms race.

In the light of such an analysis, the bishops turn to "doctrinal reflection," centering on peace and violence. Peace is linked with justice, presupposing the establishment of an order "in which men can fulfill themselves as men, where their dignity is respected, their legitimate aspirations satisfied, their access to truth recognized, their personal freedom guaranteed" (p. 76). In such a society persons will be not the objects but the agents of their own history. A crucial conclusion is drawn:

> Peace in Latin America, therefore, is not the simple absence of violence and bloodshed. Oppression by the power groups may give the impression of maintaining peace and order, but in truth it is nothing but the "continuous and inevitable seed of rebellion and war." (P. 76, citation from Pope Paul)

In addition to being a work of justice, peace is a "permanent task." It is "the result of continuous effort and adaptation to new circumstances." It is "not found, it is built," and involves a willingness to "resist personal and collective injustice." Peace, finally, is "the fruit of love," since "love is the soul of justice" (p. 77).

Such criteria are put to the test in dealing with the problem of violence. After a carefully nuanced statement, affirming with Pope Paul that "violence is neither Christian nor evangelical," that Christians prefer "peace to war," and that violent structural changes by themselves are inadequate, the report sets out its most important contribution—a new emphasis in Catholic teaching on "institutional violence," described as situations of injustice in which

> because of a structural deficiency of industry and agriculture, or national and international economy, of culture and political life, "whole towns lack necessities, live in such dependence as hinders all initiative and responsibility as well as every possibility for cultural promotion and participation in social and political life," thus violating fundamental rights. (P. 78, citation from *Populorum Progressio*, no. 30)

The above does not describe a situation of *potential* violence, but a situation of *already existing* violence. It should not be surprising, the bishops continue, that in the light of such conditions there is a temptation to what in other contexts is called counterviolence, by those whose lives are consistently violated.

Who is responsible? It is "those who have a greater share of wealth, culture and power" who are held accountable for such conditions, and are thus the real perpetrators of violence. "If they jealously retain their privileges, and defend them through violence they are responsible to history for provoking 'explosive revolutions of despair ' " (p. 79, citation from Pope Paul). Also held accountable are "those who remain passive for fear of the sacrifice and personal risk implied by any courageous and effective action" (p. 79).

A number of "pastoral conclusions" follow, including a call "to defend the rights of the oppressed," to achieve "a healthy critical sense of the social situation," to develop "grass-roots organizations," to urge a halt to the arms race, to press for "just prices for our raw materials," and "to denounce the unjust action of world powers that works against self-determination of weaker nations" (pp. 80–82).

It would be hard to overestimate the revolutionary implications of taking such a perspective seriously; much of the subsequent dedication of Latin Americans to liberation theology can be traced to this document, just as much of the nervous episcopal retreat from the implications of Medellín has centered on attempts to defuse or "spiritualize" its concerns, a matter we will examine more fully in Chapter 4.

The document contains thirty-one citations, all of them Biblical, papal, or conciliar, indicating a recognition of the importance of building on the past. And yet the document is not mere repetition of the past; it contains new insights that grow out of an analysis of the present out of which there can be a reappropriation of the past. The "reformism" of Vatican II is taking a step toward a more "revolutionary" recognition that structures deaf to the cry for justice may need to be overthrown.

If the distance between Vatican II and Medellín constitutes a step, the distance between the Medellín conference of bishops and the Santiago conference of Christians for Socialism resembles a leap.[3] Medellín was in tune with Vatican II, even if beginning to move beyond it, whereas Santiago is more self-consciously "post-conciliar." Medellín usually leans toward a "third way" between capitalism and

Marxism, whereas Santiago sees no "Christian solution," as such,
denounces the collapse into a "third way," and insists that Christians
be involved in the liberation process in socialist terms. With a few
important exceptions (such as the document on "Peace"), Medellín
speaks of inequality between persons, whereas Santiago consistently
links inequality to class struggle and the exploitation of the poor by
the rich. Medellín presses strongly for basic reform, whereas Santiago
sees no solution without revolution, not necessarily violent. Medellín
hopes that love, working for justice, can provide solutions, while
Santiago argues that love is not a historic force apart from engagement in class struggle. Medellín offers theoretical analyses of Marxism, while Santiago calls upon Christians to "form a strategic alliance
with Marxists." At Medellín the theologians were summoned by the
bishops, at Santiago they were summoned by the militant.[4]

   While some of these contrasts may be a little forced, they indicate
that real shifts can occur in less than four years. What had happened
in the interval? For one thing, Medellín unleashed a momentum that
had gradually been building and took wings after the conference. For
another, a conference on social involvement called by priests and laity
rather than bishops is almost foreordained to speak more freely and
openly. Also, the socialist option, latterly in Chile but even earlier
elsewhere, had emerged as a response to the cries of the people, and
Christians for Socialism was one response to such cries. As priests
began to identify with the poor, living and working with them, they
discovered that reformist positions were not only too slow but, because of the power ranged against them, ineffective. They also found
many of the workers already operating from a Marxist analysis; it was
not so much that the priests "took Marxism" to the workers, as that
they found Marxism already present and had to seek to relate Marxist
social analysis to Christian faith.

   A group of them, "The Eighty," issued a statement in 1971, urging
that faith in Christ be related to political commitment in socialist
terms. Out of this group evolved plans for an international conference that was held in Santiago in April 1972. The climate in Chile
was conducive to such a gathering, since at that time Allende, an
explicit Marxist, was president, having been elected in 1970 to create

a socialist society in Chile. Over four hundred Christians from Latin America and elsewhere, both Catholics and Protestants, were present, and similar conferences have subsequently been held in other parts of the world; as a result of the original Santiago meeting there is a small but growing movement of Christians for Socialism in other countries, and subsequent conferences have been held in Bologna, Ávila, and Quebec.

But not in Chile . . . The Chilean story had a tragic outcome. After the military coup in September 1973, when the junta headed by General Pinochet took control, persons publicly identified with Christians for Socialism were mercilessly tracked down; those who did not escape from the country in time were arrested, tortured, and sometimes killed. In addition, the Chilean hierarchy issued a public condemnation of the movement only a month after the coup, although the document had been prepared some time earlier.[5]

The final document of the Santiago meetings is an important one.[6] An introductory summary stresses the explicitly Christian commitments of the members of the conference, most of whom are working with the poor, and all of whom recognize that "a relatively small sector of humanity is making greater progress and growing richer every day; but the price for their progress is the oppression of two-thirds of the human race" (p. 160). The document cites imperialist capitalism as the chief cause of this situation, since it has exploited the weak for centuries and has used de facto violence to maintain control. No reformism can counter such entrenched power: "The structures of our society must be transformed from the roots up" (p. 162). The delegates therefore commit themselves to "the task of fashioning socialism [as] the only effective way to combat imperialism and to break away from our situation of dependence" (p. 163), and do so out of a clearly formulated theological and even Christological perspective.

The two main parts of the document flesh out this overall position. Part One deals with "The Latin American Reality: A Challenge for Christians" as a situation of "institutionalized violence" throughout the continent. The privileged minority willfully keep others from sharing in the fruits of their labors, and when the structures are

threatened by potential uprising, dictatorships are imposed to ensure
the preservation of the *status quo*. The reality of this class struggle
leaves only two possibilities: "dependent capitalism with its resultant
underdevelopment, or socialism" (p. 165). There can be no middle
ground, no third way, since the latter serves only to support the
destructive capitalist system. There must consequently be "a real
takeover of power by the working class" (p. 166).

The document next describes past "Attempts at Liberation in Latin
America," noting that the liberation struggle has been different in
different places, but that proponents of liberation must now unite and
overcome divisive tendencies that have left them weak and ineffective
in the past. So a choice must be made: recognizing that in the past
Christians have tended to be allied with exploiters, those at Santiago
"motivated by their faith are making a revolutionary commitment to
the people" (p. 167). This means taking political responsibility which
further means "a strategic alliance with Marxists within the liberation
process on this continent" (p. 168).

Such a conclusion leads to discussion in Part Two of "Some Aspects of Our Revolutionary Commitment," "Christianity and the
Ideological Struggle," and "Faith and Revolutionary Commitment."
In addition to generosity and goodwill, there must be a scientific
analysis of reality. Class analysis is the key to such an interpretation,
and socialism is "the only acceptable option for getting beyond a
class-based society" (p. 169). There is need "not only for a critical
theory but also for the revolutionary praxis of the proletariat" (p.
169). The presuppositions of bourgeois mentality must be unmasked
and denounced, so that the resultant change of consciousness can
lead to parties, organisms, and strategies that in turn can lead to a
takeover of power. This is not a matter of learning dogmas or parrot-
ing phrases, but of developing a critical theory that is constantly
being tested in practice. Christians have often been naive about this,
trying to deduce the specifics of a political strategy solely from "the
dignity of the human person," "love," or other such abstractions.

There is not only a socioeconomic struggle but an ideological one
as well. Human beings, for example, tend to be described in our world
as those who should "accept an already established order," and are
understood "individualistically" or "spiritualistically." But such ideo-

logical constructs, even when clothed with Christian vocabulary, turn out to be ways of sanctioning and even sanctifying the *status quo;* those who hold them unconsciously buttress the present unjust order. All of this has been part of the historic "alliance between Christianity and the ruling classes" (p. 172). Consequently, "Christians must take a definite stand on the side of the exploited in order to break this alliance" (p. 172).

Reflection on "Faith and Revolutionary Commitment" forces Christians to realize that there is a "convergence between the radicality of their faith and the radicality of their political commitment" (p. 172). There can be a fruitful interaction between the real-life presence of faith and revolutionary praxis. "Faith intensifies the demand that the class struggle move decisively towards the liberation of all men—in particular, of those who suffer the most acute forms of oppressions" (p. 172). Both faith and revolutionary commitment are bolstered *from within* this struggle with the oppressed. Faith has a critical role to play in criticizing complicity between faith and the dominant culture. But faith's reality will not come by detached theorizing; it will come only "by joining parties and organizations that are authentic instruments of the struggle of the working class" (p. 173).

The life of faith will be a life of history and conflict, a life that sees that no neutrality is possible, and recognizes that revolutionary praxis can lead to theological creativity, in which a new reading of the Bible and the Christian tradition can emerge.

Words from Ché Guevara conclude the document:

When Christians dare to give full-fledged revolutionary witness, then the Latin American revolution will be invincible; because up to now Christians have allowed their doctrine to be used as a tool by reactionaries. (P. 175)

It is out of such concerns—to see the world in the light of the gospel through the eyes of the oppressed—that liberation theology has developed in Latin America, attempting, in the words of the Santiago document, to arrive at "a new reading of the Bible and Christian tradition" (p. 174). It is time now to spell out more explicitly the theological bases of this position.

CHARACTERISTICS OF "THE VIEW FROM BELOW"

We can distinguish at least six overlapping emphases that characterize "the view from below" and differentiate it from the theology with which most of us have been familiar:

1. a different starting point: the poor
2. a different interlocutor: the nonperson
3. a different set of tools: the social sciences
4. a different analysis: the reality of conflict
5. a different mode of engagement: praxis
6. a different theology: the "second act"

Let us examine these in more detail.

1. A Different Starting Point: The Poor

Where do we begin our theological inquiry? Christian history offers many answers to this question. A favorite one starts with nature and concludes from an examination of order or beauty or causality that there must be a God. Another starts with the givenness of a set of claims made by an infallible book or an infallible church and works from that self-authenticating revelation to a world on which the revelation sheds light. A third starts with the inherently rational nature of the human mind and concludes that a universe out of which such rationality could evolve must itself be the creation of a Supreme Mind.

Liberation theology has a different starting point. Its starting point is the poor, the "marginalized," those about whom the rest of society could not care less. Dom Helder Câmara, archbishop of Recife, Brazil, has written:

> Anyone who has stood by the road trying to hitch a lift in a hurry and watched the motor cars flash by him can understand what is meant by "marginal." A marginal person is someone who is left by the wayside in the economic, social, political and cultural life of his country.[7]

The marginalized, the poor, comprise the great majority of the human family. They are not inconsequential. And it is with them that theology must start; not with theories, not with views from above, but with "the view from below." In Frederick Herzog's phrase, theology must start "where the pain is."[8]

This is not just a sociological observation. It is a theological commitment. For (as we shall see more fully in Chapter 3) liberation theology claims that it is in the life and situation of the poor that God is to be found, that God is at work. The God of the Old Testament is the God of the poor and the oppressed, a God who sides with them, taking their part and identifying with them. The God of the New Testament is the same God, a God who becomes incarnate not in one who possessed wealth or influence or a good name, but in one who belonged to the "poor of the land" (the *am ha'aretz*), a lower class/working class Jew who cast his own lot with the poor to such a consistent degree that the rich and powerful found it necessary to destroy him.

Hugo Assmann, a Brazilian theologian whose concern for the poor has led to his political exile, has used a startling expression, "the epistemological privilege of the poor," to underline the fact that the way the poor view the world is closer to the reality of the world than the way the rich view it. Their "epistemology," i.e., their way of knowing, is accurate to a degree that is impossible for those who see the world only from the vantage point of privileges they want to retain. Assmann is no romantic; when he refers to the poor, he means "the *struggling* poor," those who do not passively accept their lot as the whim of fate or the decree of a God conveniently posited as a divine sanction for those already holding power.

What conclusions follow from acknowledgment that poverty is the grinding reality of the majority of the human family? José Miguez-Bonino, a Protestant theologian, recalls some autobiographical reflections of Gustavo Gutiérrez:

> He said (in summary) I discovered three things. I discovered that *poverty was a destructive thing,* something to be fought against and destroyed, not merely something which was the object of our charity. Secondly, I discovered that *poverty was not accidental.* The fact that these people are poor and not rich is not just a matter of chance, but the result of a structure. Thirdly, I discovered that *poor people were a social class.* When I discovered that poverty was something to be fought against, that poverty was

structural, that poor people were a class [and could organize], it became crystal clear that in order to serve the poor, one had to move into political action.[9]

So the discovery of what it means to be poor can energize one into activity with and on behalf of the poor, whose problems are not solved by an occasional handout or a little organized "charity." The poor, Gutiérrez concluded, were poor not because they were lazy or "shiftless," but because society has been so structured that the poor are destined to remain poor unless they organize to change the structure of that society.

This leads to a conclusion so basic that Juan Luis Segundo, a Jesuit theologian from Uruguay, describes it as "pre-theological," i.e., available to all, whether they have theological training or not: when we take the poor as our starting point, we arrive at the conclusion that *the world should not be the way it is.* It is intolerable that

> two thirds of the human family should go to bed hungry every night,
> 15,000 people should starve to death every day,
> 20 percent of the human family should control 80 percent of the world's resources,
> human dignity should be denied to most of the human family even if they get enough to eat.

If the established harmonies of past theologies have let us remain complacent in the face of such realities, we must be suspicious of such theologies; instead of being true understandings of God and the world, they may be contrivances to ensure that the world is not basically challenged, so that those with privileges can enjoy them untroubled by uneasy consciences.

2. A Different Interlocutor: The Nonperson

A good theology does not simply set forth "a position" in a vacuum. It is a response to people's questions. Today it is the poor who are asking the questions, and it is the poor as "nonpersons" to whom we must respond, the people in society who are simply not seen, or even worse, are seen only as categories. A Chilean priest exiled from his own country because of his identification with the poor, translates the Spanish words *los pobres,* meaning "the poor (people)," as the "the poors," a category, since this is the way in which his society and ours have perceived them. His point is a profound one; when we think of "the poors" we do think of a category, i.e., of nonpersons. To speak in this way is not to make a metaphysical statement that "the poors" are not, in fact, persons, but it is to comment on a sociological reality, namely, that we perceive them as nonpersons, as those who are expendable, who can be cast aside when their "usefulness" to others has been exhausted.

There are more nonpersons in society than "the poors." North American blacks have often been treated as though they did not exist; Ralph Ellison wrote a powerful indictment of North American society from a black perspective, with the eminently appropriate title *Invisible Man.* Similarly, women have often been treated as nonpersons in a male-dominated culture. Not only have they been denied access to the male world of employment, status, privilege, and income, but the very use of language has ignored their existence. Women feel excluded when a congregation sings "Rise Up, O Men of God," or a homiletician preaches on "the brotherhood of man." That men have so much trouble understanding women's irritation at sexist language only reinforces the point. In such a milieu women are indeed nonpersons.

The theological interlocutor in the past has usually been the nonbeliever, the one for whom belief has at least become difficult. Since the time of the Enlightenment, if not before, new philosophical viewpoints and scientific world views have called into question traditional ways of speaking of God. "The world," in a phrase of Kant's that Bonhoeffer appropriated, "has come of age," it has become adult. It was Bonhoeffer's genius, as Gutiérrez himself acknowledges, to deal in a pastoral way with the intellectual questions of the nonbeliever.

But those questions in our day are the questions of a privileged minority. The real questions are being posed by the nonpersons: not questions like "How can we believe in God in an age of science?" but questions like "How can we believe in God in a society that systematically crushes and destroys us? How can we believe in God as personal when everything in the world conspires to deny our own personhood?"

It will not do to respond, "Fine! Let such people deal with such questions while we continue to respond to nonbelievers." For the nonperson as interlocutor addresses *our* theological world as well. How do *we* justify a faith that tolerates a situation where millions become nonpersons? How can *we* remain complacent in the light of structures that benefit us at the same time that they destroy others? How can *we* speak of God when our church and our nation (often working in collusion) sanction a "way of life" that expands misery rather than combatting it?

3. A Different Set of Tools: The Social Sciences

With a different starting point and a different interlocutor, it should not be surprising if we need different tools to fashion a theological response.

In the past, theological tools have usually come from philosophy. The classic case is Aquinas, who built an elaborate theological structure on the philosophy of Aristotle. Similar projects have been undertaken using Plato or Hegel or the British empiricists. And while the writings of liberation theologians are not devoid of references to Plato, Aristotle, and Hegel, the more frequently used tools of theological analysis come from the social sciences. Sociology and political science are particularly important.

Such a rejection of classical philosophy should not be surprising in a theology that starts with the poor, has the nonperson as interlocutor, and insists that the world should not be the way it is. For if Plato sees the world as a reflection of the eternal forms, if Aristotle justifies slavery, and if Hegel affirms that the Prussian state is the great achievement of humankind, it is more likely that philosophers will tend to justify the *status quo* rather than challenge it. And although sociologists and political scientists frequently defend the way things are, they also provide data that can be the raw (and even refined) material for change. If one wants to attack poverty, it is indispensable to understand the structure of a society that legitimates poverty. If one wants to challenge the right of a large nation to dominate and exploit a small nation, statistics about trade flow, tariffs, and sale of armaments are needed to buttress one's case. If one wants to examine why the few seek to retain privilege at the expense of the many, information about the economic investments of the few will help.

It is at such points that the tools of a particular form of social analysis have been of use to many liberation theologies, tools developed by an individual who happens also to have been a philosopher. The name of the individual is Karl Marx.

To many people the mere mention of Marx is enough to end the discussion. Otherwise rational minds go up the wall. This is not the place to analyze the almost pathological fear of Marx on the North American scene, particularly in church circles; to be suspected of Marxist leanings is the kiss of death in most ecclesiastical (and nonecclesiastical) establishments. But one cannot report responsibly about liberation theology without examining the impact of Marx.

Those who feel resistance should bear at least the following things in mind: *(a)* Marxism is the social reality under which millions of people live today. If some chafe under it, many others affirm it wholeheartedly and work with missionary zeal for its extension. At the very least, one has an obligation to understand a system that commands the allegiance of increasing numbers of the human family. *(b)* If Aquinas could create a medieval theology by responding to a non-Christian (Aristotle), there is no reason why theologians today could not create a contemporary Christian theology by responding to another non-Christian (Marx). *(c)* If there are facts about our world that a Marxist analysis helps us understand, we should be grateful rather than suspicious. Instead of, "Did Marx say that? If so, we must refute it," the response ought to be, "Is the analysis descriptively true? If so, let us make use of it." *(d)* The fact that Biblical insights and Marxist insights sometimes converge is no reason to discount the former. The Bible, as we will see in the next chapter, says a great deal about liberating the oppressed from the oppressors. The fact that

Marx later came to similar conclusions is not a sufficient reason to excise the concern from Christian ethics on the ground that it "sounds Marxist."

With that ground cleared, let us observe that liberation theologians have no "party line" on their relationship to Marx. We can distinguish three ways in which Marx and Marxism are appropriated:[10]

1. For some people, Marxism is a world view, an all-encompassing framework within which they make their decisions about thought and action. Such full-fledged Marxists accept a variety of insights about historical materialism, the inevitability of class struggle, religion as the opiate of the people, economic determinism, the need for armed struggle, and so forth. Such an encompassing world view works for the Marxist very much as a theological world view works for a Christian. Because the two world views make different claims about the nature of reality it would be hard for a Christian to be a Marxist *in this sense.*

2. For others, Marxism is not so much a total world view as a plan for political action. One might develop a political strategy on the basis of certain Marxist insights, for example, without being a full-fledged Marxist.

3. For still others—and, I believe, for most of the liberation theologians we are considering—Marxism is chiefly an instrument of social analysis. When they look at the world in the light of Marxist analysis, they find themselves able to understand their world better than they otherwise would. For example, if one is working with the poor in Latin America, reflection on Marx's contention that economic interests motivate our actions may help one understand (and anticipate) how multinational corporations will operate in relation to the poor. No matter what their publicity may say about "providing jobs for the poor," "raising the standard of living in Chile," or "assisting in the stabilization of the economy of Third World nations," the ultimate reason for the presence of multinational corporations is to make a profit, indeed, to make the greatest profit possible. If the choice is between paying higher wages with less profit and paying lower wages with greater profit, the latter consideration wins out, regardless of

whether or not the lower wages are enough for people to live on.

So, at any rate, a Marxist analysis would imply. Those living in such situations report that such analysis is descriptively true; the lowest wages possible are paid, and the welfare of the stockholders, rather than the welfare of the workers, remains the primary consideration. This would be part of the data with which Christians in such situations would decide how to respond to the Biblical demand for social justice.

At a recent conference composed of churchpersons from both North and South America, I was asked to prepare a short statement about some of the things we North Americans had learned. I reported in part that we now realize that we had to take both Marx and the Bible more seriously than we had before. An exiled Chilean Jesuit, who had been very active in the group known as Christians for Socialism, responded: "Why do you put Marx and the Bible right up there together? We don't equate them that way. For us, the Bible provides us with our overall approach to life, while Marx is simply a useful analytic tool within that Biblical framework. It's all right to talk about Marx if you want to, but put him in the second paragraph."

Fair enough. If one is going to use Aristotle as a tool—or Max Weber or Talcott Parsons or Peter Berger—there is no reason why Karl Marx should not also be eligible. What matters in this connection is not whether or not Marx said it, but whether or not it is descriptively true.[11]

4. A Different Analysis: The Reality of Conflict

With a different starting point, a different interlocutor, and different interpretive tools, we are likely to emerge with a different perception of the world in which we live. How does the world look when "viewed from below"?

Far from being the kind of world we wish it were (and which a "view from above" lets us imagine it really is) we discover that our world is *a world of conflict*, in which major forces are polarized and apparently unable to work together. The most frequently described polarity is that between *the oppressors and the oppressed*—a conveniently descriptive comparison that is sometimes a little slippery since those who are oppressed in one situation may become oppressors in another. It is interesting, if depressing, that those who scorn the polarity as mere rhetoric usually turn out to be comfortably situated, whereas those who affirm its descriptive truth are usually those who can easily discern the individuals and groups who are oppressing them. This is a lesson those in positions of privilege would do well to heed. There are millions who claim to be oppressed, and who can point clearly to their oppressors; this is a reality not to be scorned or slighted.

To be oppressed usually means to be in a situation of *dependency*. Oppressed persons are not the architects of their own destiny; they are economically, politically, and culturally dependent on others.[12] The decisions, for example, that affect many Latin Americans— whether they will earn enough to feed their families, whether they will live under open or repressive regimes—are less likely to be made by the people themselves than in the U.S. Department of State, or the boardroom of ITT, or the inner precincts of the Pentagon. The well-documented involvement of U.S. business and governmental interests in the overthrow of Allende in Chile in 1973 is only a single case in point. The reality of dependency only increases the power of the oppressors over the oppressed.

This means that *class struggle* may be more of a descriptive reality than we have been willing to concede. The term is usually understood as a "code word" by which to detect lurking Marxist tendencies. The fact, of course, is that Marx did not "invent" class struggle; he only reported what he saw happening, namely, that the working class tends to be relatively powerless in the face of decisions made by the ruling class, and that the place one occupies within the class structure of society tends to condition one's viewpoint. To those who see life "from below," class struggle is a patent reality. Gutiérrez speaks important words to those who deny the concept:

> When the Church rejects the class struggle, it is objectively operating as
> a part of the prevailing system. By denying the existence of social division,

this system seeks to perpetuate this division on which are based the privileges of its beneficiaries.[13]

If this is so, then it is necessary *to take sides*, since the present divisions perpetuate injustice. To be "for the oppressed" (which sounds right and proper) also means to be "against the oppressors" (which sounds divisive and threatening). The attempt *not* to take sides is in fact a decision to side with those in power, which means siding with the oppressors and thereby helping them keep control over the oppressed. There is no neutrality.

Christians often object to this line of argument. It seems to put them in the position of "stirring up trouble," or having enemies. One can respond that there has never been a time when Christians were not in the position of being called to "stir up trouble" against injustice and iniquity, and that the Christian imperative is not "Have no enemies," but rather "Love your enemies," a condition presupposing that one does indeed have enemies to love. While there is no easy prescription for loving one's enemies, it would at least involve seeing to it that enemies do not persist in acting unjustly and oppressively, since such actions dehumanize not only their victims but their perpetrators as well. Making it impossible for oppressors to continue to oppress is thus an act of love toward the oppressors as well as their victims.[14]

Christians tend to interpret evil in individualistic terms: a few bad people create the trouble, and if they can just be converted (or removed), all will be well. The truth of the matter is that *evil is systemic*—it has an uncanny way of becoming embodied in the structures of society in ways that almost give it an independent existence of its own. There can be all manner of decent people within a corporate structure, and yet evil may still be done by the structure. One can believe, for example, that the directors of Gulf and Western are decent *individuals*, who do not deliberately set out to destroy those who live in the Dominican Republic. And yet the *corporate* power of Gulf and Western does destroy many people who live in the Dominican Republic.

"Systemic evil" was not invented by liberation theologians, but it has been observed by them, since the people with whom they live and work and identify are usually its victims. For some, the recognition of systemic evil is linked with a belief that capitalism is a particularly efficient carrier of the disease. And while there is no built-in assurance that a socialist structure would be immune from such tendencies, the baleful effects that have been observed in the life of the poor under capitalist economies in the Third World have led many to entertain a socialist option more willingly than they might otherwise have done. And for this reality the injustices of capitalism are at least as responsible as the logic of Marx.

If the world is even partially the way it is pictured above, a question is posed for us: Why is it that we fail to perceive the world as it truly is? The answer such an analysis forces on us goes: *We fail to perceive the world this way because such an admission would be too costly for us.* It would mean jeopardizing our privileges, our power, and our influence; it would mean questioning our right to many of our comforts, since they are procured at the cost of exploiting those who produce them and cannot afford such comforts for themselves. Two devastating lines in a song by Al Carmines drive the point home:

> And slowly outrage turns to resignation
> And comfort makes a truce with indignation.[15]

One can offer this disturbing answer either from a belief that human judgments are economically determined (e.g., that we filter truth in ways congenial to our pocketbooks) or from a traditional and orthodox belief that we operate out of sinful self-interest, whether economically motivated or not. In either case, a bias toward self-enhancement at great cost to other selves remains.

5. A Different Mode of Engagement: Praxis

It is not helpful to end on a negative note. Are there ways to become engaged and work for change?

At this point our tidy scheme begins to buckle, for what is now point 5 could just as well have been point 1. The point of point 5 is that there is no true theology without engagement; theology must both *issue from* engagement and *lead to* renewed engagement. The word that encompasses this double movement is in danger of becoming a fad word, but we must use it even so, since there is nothing that quite takes its place. The word is praxis, and it means something different from the familiar-sounding "practice." Praxis describes the two-way traffic, or better stated, the circular traffic that is always going on between action and theory.

Action forces me to look at theory again. (Is how I perceive the world before I acted the way the world really is? Well, no, not quite; because of my action I now see the world differently and must act differently as a result.) *And theory forces me to look at action again.* (Am I acting in the most effective manner, the world being the way I now perceive it? Well, no, not quite; so because of a modified theory I must now act differently and see the world differently as a result.)

This is a never-ending process. It is my participation in a process of seeking to transform society. Because it is not merely cerebral but action-oriented as well, some are insisting (in a jaw-breaking distinction) that the Christian's task is not "ortho-doxy," e.g., right thinking, but "ortho-praxis," e.g., the right combination of thinking and doing.

To take praxis seriously means, therefore, that we know the truth in a different way. It is not a matter of applying timeless truths to a finished universe we cannot understand without their help. Rather, both our understanding and our world remain unfinished; each needs development and refinement in relation to the other. As Gutiérrez puts it, "Knowledge is not the conformity of the mind to the given, but an immersion in the process of transformation and construction of a new world."[16] This, too, is an ongoing task, involving our constant check of action at the hand of theory, theory at the hand of action. It confirms the ongoing truth of Marx's eleventh thesis against Feuerbach, in which he claims that the task is not to understand the world but to change it, not to have a passive intellectual acceptance *of* something, but an ongoing dialectical relationship *with* something, in interchange with which both it and we are transformed.

For the Christian, praxis is the means by which we attempt to work with God in building "the new heaven and the new earth." It is not simply any kind of action in tension with theory, but *transforming action,* transforming action finally by the poor and humiliated. As Gregory Baum has put it, praxis involves "a total dynamics of historical vision and social transformation. . . . Praxis is the precondition of knowledge, even though in turn this knowledge issues forth in a new praxis."[17]

So we begin to discern a content to praxis, although it is not a content neatly determined in advance; it will grow out of, respond to, condition and be conditioned by, the situation. But since it is praxis committed to the poor and to the transformation of the world, undertaken from "the view from below," we can describe it, in the precise technical meaning of the word, as *subversive action. Vertir* means "to overthrow, to turn upside down." The Christians described in Acts 17:6 fit this very well: "Those who have turned the world upside down" is the way they were pictured. But from what stance does one turn the world upside down? There are two possibilities: one would be *super-version,* turning the world upside down "from above," for the benefit of the affluent and the powerful; the other possibility would be *sub-version,* turning the world upside down "from below," for the benefit of the poor and powerless. Christian praxis is clearly sub-version, transformation "from below," on behalf of, but finally by, "the wretched of the earth," the poor and dispossessed.[18]

6. A Different Theology: The "Second Act"

If we can understand the emphasis on praxis, it will be easier to understand the role of theology. In a phrase that Gutiérrez uses frequently, theology is "critical reflection on praxis." It is our attempt to reflect on what goes on in the praxis situation. It is not a theory we impose on our life and our world, to which we expect our life and our world to conform; it is our way of thinking, as Christians, about what is going on in that life and that world. This means, in another phrase Gutiérrez has popularized, that theology is always the "second act." The "first act" is *commitment,* the personal decision we make with our whole being to be available to God and the world for the transformation of the world on behalf of, and alongside, the poor— which is another way of saying "on behalf of, and alongside" God, since God is found among the poor. The second act is our reflection on what transpires because of the first act. It is not so much a theology from above as a theology from below, from within the situation. It is our attempt to reflect on praxis undertaken within "the view from below." In one sense this is a very classical, and hardly original, view of theology, which could be likened to the Anselmic understanding of "faith seeking understanding," in which commitment likewise comes first. The difference, of course, has to do with the *context* in which the commitment is made.

Such a theology will have numerous resources: one will be the situation itself, another will be the commitment we bring to the situation, a third will be the heritage we have inherited through the Scriptures and the tradition (which we will explore in Chapter 3), while a fourth will be the community called church within which we move and live and think and worship and act (and which we will explore in Chapter 6).

It is important to take account of these other things since the discussion thus far might suggest that we are dealing chiefly with politics and economics. It has been necessary to stress politics and economics since they are so often slighted in other theological discussions. But a theology of liberation is always more than that. It will have at least three emphases: *(a)* It is the aspiration of oppressed people to escape from the destruction that is part of their everyday life, to get free from that kind of oppression. *(b)* It is also, however, an understanding of history in which people can realize that they can take a conscious responsibility for their own destiny. This is particularly important in cultures that have implied that if you are poor, that is the way God meant it to be, and that if you endure your lot quietly, you will be rewarded in another world—a theology calculated to draw warm support from all those presently in power. This recognition that there are possibilities for changing the world, and that God empowers people to work for justice, is crucial. *(c)* The liberation that comes is a transformation made possible through encounter with Jesus

Christ, who liberates from sin and for freedom. This involves a recognition, however, that sin is not just private, inward and personal, but also the alienation to which our whole society has been subjected. Not only do we sin against one another individually, we perpetuate those sins corporately through structure whose ongoing existence militates against humanizing possibilities for others.

Full liberation, full freedom in Christ, will involve not just escape from oppressive structures, not just acknowledging history as an arena of human responsibility, not just recognition that personal sins are forgiven, but a mix of all three.[19]

A NOTE STILL TO BE SOUNDED

Those are a half dozen emphases that characterize "theology in a new key," a theology of liberation, and distinguish it from some of the established harmonies in which we have ordinarily done theology.

But a further note has not yet been sounded, not because it is unimportant, but because it is too important to receive brief treatment. This is the use which liberation theology makes of Scripture (and, through Scripture, the whole Christian tradition). Since concern for Scripture is shared by all Christians, in whatever key their theologies are pitched, an examination of the approach to Scripture can help us to join the issues even more decisively.

CHAPTER 3

The Melodic Stridency of Scripture: Marx, Luke, and John

(From a Hermeneutic of Suspicion to a Hermeneutic of Engagement)

> By understanding biblical theological ideology as timely perception rather than timeless truth we can engage in a real conversation with the Bible.
> —*Joe Hardegree, in* The Bible and Liberation, *a "Radical Religion" Reader, p. 169*

> The quartet played Brahms. Brahms lost.
> —*News item*

Should we speak of the "melodic stridency" or the "strident melody" of Scripture? Following the rule that the noun should control the adjective, it might seem more appropriate to talk about Scripture having a *melody* that is occasionally strident, rather than the other way around. However, the melody of Scripture is so familiar, and the phrases attached to it so sonorous, that we can almost always assimilate the stridency without being upset by it. The harsh and demanding quality of the Biblical message escapes us; we find the melody beautiful rather than strident.

If, on the other hand, we emphasize the *stridency,* the harshness, of Scripture, a stridency that is occasionally melodic, we will not be lulled by sweet and familiar sounds, but continually caught off guard

by unexpected and challenging ones. We will be more likely to hear
Scripture on its terms, rather than using it as an echo chamber for
ours. Our established harmonies will be more susceptible to transposition into the new key of Biblical declaration.

THE BENEFICIAL EFFECTS OF STRIDENCY

Sometimes it is only after the intrusion of stridency that our ears
are opened to hear the melody *in the way it is meant to be heard.*
Stridency, dissonance, discord can sometimes give new meaning to
the melody. Two musical examples can illustrate the point.

The Welsh hymn tune *Rhosymedre* is not, by most standards of
musical accountability, particularly distinguished. The melody is predictable, the harmonies are ordinary, there are few surprises. But
Ralph Vaughan Williams has composed an organ chorale-prelude on
the tune, creating an embroidery of discord, dissonance, and unexpected juxtapositions of notes and rhythms that, albeit in a quiet way,
is strident. The piece is exciting not only in its own right but because
of what it does to the original melody. For when one goes back and
listens once again to the melody, *it is transformed.* The notes are the
same, of course, but that which was banal is now fresh and new.

Something similar occurs in the final movement of Sibelius' *Fifth
Symphony.* The main theme is a series of unoriginal block chords that
simply bounce up and down, monotonously repeated and repeated
and repeated; even when another melody begins to be woven over
them, their predictable repetition is almost maddening. But toward
the end of the movement Sibelius begins to experiment. He gives the
chords striking new harmonies, harsh harmonies, strident harmonies,
within which he weaves new patterns, stretching his musical idiom
almost to the breaking point, through measure after measure of
unresolved discords that are only, after agonized strain, finally resolved. And once again, having heard the stridency, we discover that
the old chords are now heard in a new way, no longer banal and
predictable, but latent with new possibilities for which the listener
is prepared on each rehearing of the symphony.

These are at least faint analogies for what can happen when the familiar melodies of Scripture confront us in (what seem initially to be) strident resettings. We discover that the stridency is part of the Biblical message itself, which, freed from the safe interpretive shell in which we had encased it, speaks to us in fresh, albeit threatening, fashion, in ways with which we are forced to come to terms. We hear things we had not heard before, *even though the words are the same as they always were.*

This is part of what liberation theologians can do for us—as we observe what *they* hear in the Biblical text (frequently so different from what we have heard) we are "liberated" to hear what we had not heard before. It does not mean that the Bible's message to us will be the same as the Bible's message to them, for it speaks in different ways to people in different situations. It does mean, however, that the Bible's message to us will now be different. For they will have forced us to confront the stridency from which we had previously insulated ourselves.

Recognizing Our "Ideological Captivity"

Why have we heard only certain things in Scripture, and been attuned only to smooth melodies rather than strident discords? To explore this question involves a discussion of "ideology," which is a reality in our lives whether we have been aware of it or not.

In 1975, I attended a conference of North and South Americans at which there were a number of theologians. After three or four days, one of the Latin-American theologians said to us, "Why is it that when you talk about our position you always describe it as 'Latin-American theology,' but when you talk about *your* position you always describe it as 'theology'?"

A salutary question. For although we would all have denied it, we were in fact assuming that *our* position was normative ("pure" theology untainted by geographical or class biases), whereas *their* position was derivative (theology conditioned by the fact that it was being done in Latin America), a variant on the true theological position, namely ours.

It was true, of course, that their theology was conditioned by the

fact that it was being done in Latin America, in situations of oppression, in culturally Catholic settings, chiefly by men who were incor-
porating Marxist analysis into their theological formulations. We saw
all those limiting factors very clearly. What we failed to see (until our
friendly questioner forced us to see it) was that our theology was just
as culturally conditioned as theirs: it was being done in North America, in situations of affluence, in culturally pluralistic settings, chiefly
by men (though now and again by women), who were importing
capitalist assumptions into their theological formulations.

In that situation, we North Americans were illustrating our "ideological captivity." Without even knowing it, we were allowing our
ideas, even our theology, to be formed and conditioned by particular
mind-sets or points of view, which inevitably colored (and distorted)
those ideas and that theology. What we *brought to* our thinking
massively influenced what we *took from* it. The fact that we were
unaware of all this only underlines how deep our ideological captivity
was.

The meaning of "ideology" is as complicated as it is important. On
one level, it has an almost neutral meaning, standing for any system
of ideas expressing a particular point of view about reality. On this
level, everyone has an ideology; it may be a Marxist ideology, a
bourgeois ideology, a working-class ideology, a fascist ideology, a
communitarian ideology. On this level also we can speak of the
ideology of an age or epoch—one era is a time of "the failure of
nerve," another of the reassertion of individualism. It is in this sense
that Juan Luis Segundo uses the term in *The Liberation of Theology:*

> By "ideology" here I am simply referring to the system of goals and means
> that serves as the necessary backdrop for any human option or line of
> action.[1]

But ideology is more frequently used in a pejorative sense. We talk
about ideology as a rationalization of self-interest, a means by which
one group seeks to justify its control over another. When we distrust
the reasons behind someone else's action we often describe those
reasons as ideological, and claim that the reasons publicly offered hide
or obfuscate the *true* reasons for the action. Refusing to take the
offered reasons at face value, we look behind or around them for

motivations that will better account for the action. As Karl Mann-heim puts it:

> The concept "ideology" reflects the one discovery which emerged from political conflict, namely, that ruling groups can in their thinking become so intensively interest-bound to a situation that they are simply no longer able to see certain facts which would undermine their sense of domi-nation. There is implicit in the word "ideology" the insight that in certain situations *the collective unconscious of certain groups obscures the real condition of society both to itself and others and thereby stabilizes it.* [2]

This bending of the evidence, in an effort to make reality conform to what one wants reality to be, is a prevailing tendency of ideological thought, and suggests that ideology will work on the side of conform-ity, of maintenance of things as they are, particularly as it is employed by those in power. Mannheim, in fact, posits as a characteristic of ideology that it will be directed "toward the maintenance of the existing order," and that ideas driving toward change in the existing order should be labeled by contrast as "utopian."

For a theologian like Gutiérrez, therefore, ideology must be chal-lenged, since

> it spontaneously fulfills a function of preservation of the established order.
> . . . This does not mean that ideology cannot place the existing order into a relationship with ideals which are not found within it: but what is characteristic of ideology is that it does so in such a way that those ideals do not provoke real change in the established order. [3]

Certain conclusions from this brief discussion are relevant to our approach to Scripture:

1. All of us have certain ideological assumptions; no one thinks in "pure" or disinterested categories.
2. Most of us use our ideologies to rationalize keeping things as they are, particularly when things are working to our benefit. We detect this propensity more easily in others than in ourselves.
3. Our reasons for affirming what we affirm are thus always open to suspicion.
4. It is our failure to acknowledge points 1–3 that constitutes our "ideological captivity."
5. We begin to recognize our ideological captivity when confronted

with *another* way of viewing reality sufficiently at variance with our own to force us to take the other view seriously, thereby challenging the adequacy of our own position.

6. As we observe the responses of liberation theologians to Scripture we are forced to reexamine our own responses to Scripture. This is the beginning of our liberation from "ideological captivity." It involves what Segundo calls "ideological suspicion," i.e., a recognition that our positions are products of intellectual manipulation. Any ideology that allows us to juxtapose an outraged recognition that "there is monstrous evil in the world" with the complacent conclusion, "I am satisfied that the world should not basically change," must arouse suspicion. Only out of such suspicion can the chains of ideological captivity be smashed.

"Hermeneutical Suspicion"

"Hermeneutics" is almost as forbidding a technical term as "ideology"; it is nevertheless useful in a nontechnical discussion. "Hermeneutics" (coming from a Greek verb meaning "to make clear") simply means the science of interpreting texts. Whenever I begin a sentence with the words "What the author means is . . .," I am engaging in a hermeneutical exercise. I may offer a good interpretation or a bad one, but at least it will be interpretation, hermeneutics.

We have already referred to "ideological suspicion" as the need to suspect ideologies that permit us to remain complacent in the face of human suffering. What is the source of an ideology that does not combine moral outrage with a desire to transform the world so that hunger and misery are no more? Such an ideology can only be shaped in situations where the shapers are either insulated from such ugly realities, or are so enamored of their comfort that they avoid challenges that would threaten their comfort.

Much the same thing is true, as Segundo notes, when we turn from confronting the world to confronting Scripture. And it is the moral passion of Segundo, Gutiérrez, Miranda, and other Third World theologians in confronting Scripture that forces us to move from ideological suspicion to hermeneutical suspicion: if indeed "the world should not be the way it is," how is it that we can encounter Scripture (committed to the "creation of a new heaven and a new earth") without being moved by that encounter to engage in such transforming activity? How adequate is our hermeneutics, our method of interpretation, if it leaves us complacent with the way things are, or committed only to tepid changes that fall far short of the Bible's radical demand for justice? Must we not engage in hermeneutical suspicion as well?

Hermeneutical suspicion will force us to confront such questions as the following:

> Since the God of the Bible is on the side of the poor, why are we undisturbed by the fact that we are among the nonpoor?
>
> Since the God of the Bible cries out for justice, why are we such complacent recipients of goods that are gotten unjustly?
>
> Since the God of the Bible yearns for peace, why are we so untroubled by constant preparation for war?
>
> Since the God of the Bible decries worship that is oblivious to the plight of the stranger "outside the gate," why do we enter our sanctuaries oblivious to the human destruction outside those sanctuaries?
>
> Since the God of the Bible wills that all be fed, how can we feel right about consuming 40 percent of the world's resources when we are only 6 percent of the world's population?

It is clear that there are some selective lenses by means of which we read Scripture, and that those lenses need to be torn from our eyes. One reason we can read Scripture complacently is that we approach it selectively. We read what we can bear to read, we hear what is tolerable to hear, and we evade (or "spiritualize") those parts which leave us uncomfortable, if not outraged. What we *bring to* Scripture, in other words, conditions what we *draw from* Scripture: our ideology is transplanted into our hermeneutic, so that there is a double distortion, and therefore double cause for suspicion.

So subtly does this happen that the point must be pressed, if we are to hear liberation theologians responding to the Biblical message.

Let us take a Biblical passage that speaks to Third World peoples in their situations of captivity and oppression, and observe how we transform its message. The passage is the episode in Luke 4:16–30, in which Jesus returns to Nazareth and preaches on the famous passage in Isaiah 61 describing "the year of the Lord," which Jesus says has come to fulfillment through his proclamation. The content as Luke reports it is as follows:

> The Spirit of the Lord is upon me,
> because he has anointed me to preach
> good news to the poor.
> He has sent me to proclaim
> release to the captives,
> and recovering of sight to the blind,
> to set at liberty
> those who are oppressed,
> to proclaim the acceptable year of the Lord.[4]

To victims of economic poverty and political oppression, the message would seem eminently straightforward, particularly when the reference to "the acceptable year of the Lord" was known to describe the jubilee, a time of economic restitution, when debts would be canceled, and seized lands would revert to their former owners.

But that is a radical message, upsetting the *status quo*, and threatening those in power—whether in Jesus' day or our own. How do we handle such a text so that its message becomes nonthreatening? We do this by letting our ideology shape our hermeneutic. Here are some examples that should surely engender hermeneutical suspicion.

The author of the Moffatt Bible Commentary on Luke writes:

> On Jesus' lips the "good news" has a purely religious import. . . . The term *the poor* is to be taken in its inward spiritual sense .   . and similarly the expressions *captive, blind, oppressed* indicate not primarily the down-trodden victims of material force, such as Rome's, but the victims of inward repressions, neuroses, and other spiritual ills due to misdirection and failure of life's energies and purposes.[5]

The commentator in *The Interpreter's Bible* exegetes the verse "He has sent me to proclaim release to the captives" as follows:

The captivity referred to is evidently moral and spiritual. Thought is not moving now on the plane of opening the doors of physical jails, but rather of setting men free from the invisible but terribly real imprisonment into which their souls may fall.[6]

A similar tendency can be observed in the treatment of other Lucan passages that are read by Third World Christians as full of revolutionary import. The language of the Magnificat (to which we shall return at the end of this chapter and which contains such lines as "He has put down the mighty from their thrones, and exalted those of low degree; he has filled the hungry with good things, and the rich he has sent empty away") is dealt with as follows:

> This language, *though it is not to be taken literally but in a spiritual sense*, shows how intimately in Judaic Christianity the coming of the Christ still stirred the chords of national hope.[7]

In his treatment of the Beatitudes, describing the "Realm of God," the author writes:

> Many, doubtless, of Jesus' hearers had come to think of that Realm in terms of liberation from the foreign yoke of Rome and the restoration of national glory, but Jesus lays *all* the emphasis on the spiritual or inward character of redemption.[8]

Of course there is some truth in those assessments; Jesus was concerned about the inner spiritual dimension of human existence as well as the other physical, political-social dimensions. And there is evidence even within the Gospels of attempts to mute the stress on the poor. In Luke, the point is clear: it is *"you poor"* who are directly addressed in the Beatitudes, with no equivocation. In Matthew it has become not only *"the* poor" but "the poor *in spirit"*—already two stages removed from the Lucan immediacy (cf. Luke 6:20 and Matt. 5:3). But the interpreters, dealing with the Lucan passage alone, insist that Jesus was concerned *only* with the "inward, spiritual sense," with "the spiritual or inward character of redemption," and so on. The consistency with which Jesus' message is confined to the "inward" and "spiritual" is astounding. The harsh, angular, strident, and threatening implications of the passages have been successfully muted: one need not be upset by them nor view them as a threat to the way things are.

It is possible to respond: "But you are just as one-sided as those you attack. Who says Jesus is preaching revolutionary politics rather than inward peace? Isn't your bias just as pronounced as theirs?" This is a fair question, a reply to which will emerge as the rest of the chapter unfolds. But the question even at this stage reminds us that *everyone* brings a bias to the reading of Scripture, just as the Biblical writers themselves brought a bias to the texts they created. So the task, in Biblical interpretation, will not be to seek a "bias-free" vantage point, but to seek to make one's own bias come as close to that of the Scriptures as possible.

Let us therefore draw some conclusions about the need for ideological and hermeneutical suspicion if we are to be open to the insights of others:

1. *What we see is not necessarily what is there.* For example, during a recent trip to Chile and Argentina, my wife and I spent several days in Buenos Aires. The city is cultured, charming, "European," bustling but tranquil. That is what we "saw." But what is really "there" is a police state; late at night on those same bustling streets people are taken from their homes by masked gangs. They are never heard from again; they become "the disappeared," who are tortured to extract information about their political activities before they are killed.

2. *What we see depends on where we are standing.* We saw things one way in Buenos Aires; government officials see them differently, while the families of "the disappeared" see them in another way. If we employ a different image, where the horizon is depends on whether we are standing on a beach a few feet above sea level or two thousand feet high on a coastal range. Put still another way, a plate of food will mean one thing to an affluent resident of Buenos Aires who sees it at 11 P.M. after having finished a sumptuous meal; it will mean something entirely different to an impoverished resident of Buenos Aires who has not eaten for three days.

3. *When others tell us what they see, we need to know where they are standing as well as where we are standing.* Upon our return from South America, we received a letter from a group that supports the

military junta in Chile, assuring us that reports about "political prisoners" in Chile were not only exaggerated but untrue, since there was
"full political freedom in Chile," people were smiling on the streets,
no one was afraid, and the junta had worked an economic miracle.
This was an absolute contradiction of what we had observed only a
few weeks earlier, noting the widespread activity of the DINA (the
secret police), the massive hunger of the poor, especially of children,
and the high incidence of "the disappeared." Knowing that the letter
came from a Washington lobby trying to improve the image of the
junta and secure U.S. Government and business support for it, was
important evidence in our assessment of the degree of its accuracy.
(The writer of the letter would be similarly suspicious of any reports
we made about conditions in Chile.)

4. *No matter how much anybody sees, nobody sees it all.* By now,
this should be a self-evident truth. It means that we need help from
all sources in putting together an accurate picture of what is really
going on.

All of which leads to a self-evident conclusion:

5. *What we see is always subject to correction.* The application of
these insights to Biblical interpretation should also verge on the
self-evident. What we hear in a Biblical text may not actually be what
the text is saying. What we hear depends in part on the viewpoint
we bring to the text, and this will also be true of what others hear
in the text; to know their viewpoint will help us to assess their
interpretation. And since nobody can possibly hear everything, we
need not only to listen to what others hear but to be open to correction in the light of what they tell us.

"HERMENEUTICAL CIRCULATION"

There is a further step. In confronting Scripture we are not only
dealing with different interpretations in our own historical situation,
we are also dealing with texts that came out of historical situations
of their own. Thus our task is to find the correct interplay between
the text in *its* historical situation and what it says to us in *our*
historical situation.

There are, as we have already seen, numerous ways to cheat in this enterprise. We can dehistoricize the text so that it becomes a "timeless truth" rather than a "timely perception" (making "the poor you have always with you" an excuse for complacency); we can emphasize the text's historical context so much that its impact is lost on us (making "if any man ask you to go with him one mile, go with him two" an outmoded requirement of first-century military law); or we can let our own historical situation smother the text (making Jesus' query, "Wist ye not that I must be about my Father's business?" a Biblical endorsement of free enterprise).

To diminish either the temptation or the ability to cheat, we need, first, to keep alive a back-and-forth tension between the text and ourselves, and second (a point to which we shall return) to do so as communally as possible, since improbable individual interpretations can sometimes be corrected under the discipline of community judgment. The exciting fact today is that we are beginning to listen to Christians in other parts of the world as well as our own, and to those in our part of the world who come from other social, racial, and class situations than ours—all trying to relate our diverse situations to identical texts.

The back-and-forth exercise referred to above is often described as "the hermeneutical circle." Partly because the imagery of "circle" is static (the circle is the perfect and finished figure), we shall employ instead a phrase suggested by the French theologian Georges Casalis and refer to "hermeneutical circulation." This more dynamic term describes the reality we experience—an ongoing "circulation" from text to self to text again, from past historical context to present historical context and back again. As José Miguez-Bonino, an Argentinian theologian, has put it, the circulation is "between the text in its historicity and our own historical reading of it in obedience."[9]

The back-and-forthness applies to the entire theological enterprise. As Gutiérrez makes clear, what we are calling "hermeneutical circulation" is always a two-way street,

> . . . from humanity to God and from God to humanity; from history to faith and from faith to history; from the human word to the word of the Lord and from the word of the Lord to the human word; from human love

to the love of God and from the love of God to human love; from human justice to the holiness of God and from the holiness of God to human justice; from the poor to God and from God to the poor.[10]

To be faithful to such dynamics means a recognition of the following:

a. a text (let us say, the writings of a prophet);
b. the historical situation of the text (let us say, a time of oppression);

and

c. our own interpretation of a and b, that is to say, of the text in its situation.

So far so good. But there are some complicating factors:

d. our own historical situation *as seen by us* (let us say, not a time of oppression but of prosperity, which will condition how we approach the text, what we look for in it, what we hear it saying, and so forth);

along with:

e. our own historical situation *as seen by others* (let us say, those who live under an oppression similar to that under which the Biblical writer lived, and who feel that our prosperity is made possible by our exploitation of them);

not to mention:

f. our own historical situation as seen by us once we have listened to the others—so that we now see the text in a new way and thus *approach our own historical situation in a newer way still;*

or:

g. our own historical situation as seen by us once we have listened to the others—so that we now see our situation in a new way and thus *approach the text in a new way;*

which brings us back to a and enables us to start the process all over again.

So it is not just a matter of ourselves and the text, it is a matter of ourselves *and others* and the text. The others are needed to tell us not only how they perceive the text but also how they perceive us perceiving the text (a service we must also perform for them). It is out of this mutual search, mutual interpretation, and mutual correction that we can create a new hermeneutic.

A HERMENEUTIC OF HOPE

Beatriz Melano Couch, an Argentinian theologian steeped in the hermeneutical insights of Paul Ricoeur and her own experiences in South America, takes the argument a step farther by insisting that we move beyond a hermeneutic of suspicion to a hermeneutic of hope, which can also be described as a hermeneutic of engagement. It is a hermeneutic of hope because "it hopes to avoid . . . the danger of reading into the text only our own conditioning, with the aim of freeing the text, letting the text speak with all its urgency, depth and power."[11]

Once this liberation from ideological captivity has occurred, a second contribution of the hermeneutic of hope will emerge: "Then it hopes to let the text itself rephrase our own questions and rephrase our own conceptions about life and death, our own epistemology, our own knowledge of society, our ethics [and] politics."[12]

A third characteristic may be added to the two she has noted: the content of the emerging message will not be one of immobilizing despair but of liberating hope. The Biblical message is not just No but also Yes; not just destruction of the old but also creation of the new; not just threat but also promise; not just negation but also fulfillment.

Let us see how this works, by examining some Biblical passages that have been central to Third World Bible study, highlighting emphases that we, in our ideological captivity, are likely to have missed.[13]

1. The God Who Takes Sides
(Exodus 1:8–14; 2:23–25; 3:7–10ff.)

If there is a single passage that encapsulates the liberation themes of the Bible, it is the exodus story, describing a God who takes sides, intervening to free the poor and oppressed. Let us look at the story on three successive levels:

If we listen to the story as much as possible on its own terms, we hear at least the following things:

The Israelites are being oppressed and the Egyptians are oppressing them. Not only are things tough, they continually get tougher; complaints lead to new burdens rather than to relief. (Ch. 1:8–14.) But the Israelites are not alone. God hears the groaning of the people, and remembers the covenant earlier made with them. (Ch. 2:23–25.)

More than that, God takes sides, declaring that the people will be liberated from their oppressors. Moses is delegated to lead the people out of their bondage, and after many trials the liberation is accomplished. (Ch. 3:7–10ff.)

So much is clear from the story itself, apart from special pleading or partisan manipulation.

As Third World Christians hear the story in their situation, but still focusing on the story itself, what do they hear? Something hopeful. It goes something like this: It is good news to hear that God takes sides and does not remain aloof from situations of human misery. It is even better news to hear that God takes sides with the oppressed, not only siding *with* Israel but *against* Pharaoh, since these are clear conditions for Israel's liberation. It may be the best news of all to hear that Israel's liberation is not just liberation from individual sin and guilt (important as that is) but liberation from the oppressive political and economic structures that have been destroying the Israelites. Inescapable conclusion: God has a concern with the quality of political and economic structures.

Let us listen to the story once more, as Third World Christians reflect on what it says to them *in their situation today*. At least three things emerge:

a. If the God of the story is a living God, then God *still takes sides*. Elementary.

b. If God takes sides today, it is still with the oppressed, the poor, the downtrodden. This means that God is against the Pharaohs of this world, the modern exploiters. And who are "the Pharaohs of this world" today? It is not hard for the oppressed to identify them: they are the tiny minority at home who are in collusion against the great majority; they are churches and churchpersons who give support to such oligarchies; and they are the rich and powerful from other nations who keep national oligarchies in power, thereby becoming complicit in the ongoing exploitation of the poor. Let us not be deceived: the latter, before the analysis goes much farther, will include North American businessmen, the State Department, the Pentagon, the CIA, and those who by votes and taxes keep such groups in power. From the perspective of oppressed people and the exodus story, we are the servants in Pharaoh's court.

c. Today also God liberates not only from personal sin and guilt but also from the structures of the world that are evil, exploitive, and unjust. That is the promise of the story. So today also God has a concern with the quality of our political and economic structures. Those who seek to help God must respond to those structures, siding with whatever forces are working for liberation, opposing whatever forces continue to exploit and destroy.

The story proclaims hope to the oppressed and judgment to the oppressors. To those who serve in Pharaoh's court, the message is strident. It leaves little doubt where most of us are located.

2. "To Know God Is to Do Justice"
(Jeremiah 22:13–16)

Many liberation theologians affirm that a major message of the Bible goes: "To know God is to do justice." This pervasive theme can be illustrated with dozens of texts; a particularly compelling one is found in Jeremiah. The prophet, speaking for Jahweh, is inveighing against the king (a favorite pastime of prophets); the king is exploiting his subjects by inordinate personal demands at the cost of great oppression to everyone else:

> Shame on the man who builds his house by non-justice,
> and completes its upstairs rooms by non-right,
> who makes his fellow man work for nothing,
> without paying him his wages,
> who says, "I will build myself an imposing palace
> with spacious rooms upstairs,"
> who sets windows in it,
> panels it with cedar, and paints it vermillion.

He then compares the king unfavorably to his father, who, without being an ascetic (he "ate and drank like you"), still embodied justice rather than injustice:

> Are you more of a king
> for outrivalling others with cedar?
> Your father ate and drank like you,
> but he practiced justice and right;
> this is good.
> He defended the cause of the poor and needy;
> this is good.

The culmination of the passage is pointed. Referring to the practice of justice and right, the defense of the poor and needy, a question is posed:

> Is this not what it means to know me? It is
> Jahweh who speaks.[14]

The question is rhetorical. This *is* "what it means to know [Jahweh]," i.e., to practice justice and right, to defend the cause of the poor and needy. To know God is not to engage in private piety or subscribe to certain orthodox statements or worship correctly on the Sabbath. *To know God is to do justice.* Conversely, the sign of not knowing God is to do injustice. The one who does injustice not only incurs the "shame" with which the passage opens but is, in effect, an atheist, denying God by the quality of life that puts having a beautiful palace above concern for persons.

The conviction that "to know God is to do justice" gives added power to a later passage in Jeremiah, describing the "new covenant" that Jahweh will make with his people (Jer. 31:31–34), the distinguishing feature of which is that "no longer shall each man teach his neighbor and teach his brother, saying, 'Know the Lord,' for *they shall all know me,* from the least of them to the greatest, says the Lord" (v. 34, italics added). This is noble and even inspiring rhetoric, but when we relate the two Jeremiah passages we realize that the equation between knowing God and doing justice transforms the "new covenant" from a beautiful dream to a stern demand: the "new covenant" between Jahweh and the people means a situation where the doing of justice is the order of the day.

We can take it one step farther. At the Last Supper, Jesus makes explicit reference to the Jeremiah passage about the "new covenant," asserting that "this cup which is poured out for you is the new covenant in my blood" (Luke 22:20; cf. Matt. 26:28; Mark 14:24; I Cor. 11:23). The future hope of Jeremiah's time has become a present reality in Jesus' time: God can *now* be "known." In the light of Jeremiah 22, however, we realize that Jesus is not offering mere information about cosmic reality, but empowerment to "do justice," for that is what it means to "know God" under the terms of the "new covenant" his death ushers in. This makes participation in the Lord's Supper a "political" act—an acceptance of the doing of justice as the way to know God. To gather for nourishment at the Lord's Table, unconcerned about the lack of nourishment on so many other tables, is not only hypocrisy but profanation—a denial of the very covenant it is meant to celebrate.

3. The True Worship
(Isaiah 58:6–7)

Not only is knowledge of God predicated on the doing of justice, but (as our comments on the Lord's Supper have anticipated) the worship of God must be an expression of justice. This theme is most familiar in The Book of Amos, with its famous denunciation of cultic practices that are offered in lieu of the creation of a just social order: God speaks:

> I hate, I despise your feasts,
> and I take no delight in your solemn assemblies. . . .
> Take away from me the noise of your songs;
> to the melody of your harps I will not listen.
> But let justice roll down like waters,
> and righteousness like a mighty stream.
> (Amos 5:21, 23–24)

Miranda argues that the prophetic message is that *until* there is justice there should be no worship, no cult. The message of Amos can be summarized, Miranda claims, as: "I do not want cultus but rather interhuman justice." In Isa. 1:1–20, Jahweh asserts that he will no longer hear the prayers of the people; instead of praying, they should "search for justice [and] help the oppressed." The New Testament has a similar message encapsulated in I John 4:7–8: "He who does not love does not know God." If we do not love the neighbor whom we have seen, how can we love God whom we have not seen?

Such concerns are not theoretical; Camilo Torres, a priest in Colombia, finally stopped exercising his priestly duties since they seemed to him a diversion from identifying with those who were trying to create a more just social order:

> I have ceased to say Mass [in order] to practice love for people in temporal, economic and social spheres. When the people have nothing against me, when they have carried out the revolution, then I will return to offering Mass, God willing. I think that in this way I follow Christ's injunction ". . . leave thy gift upon the altar and go first to be reconciled to thy brothers [and sisters]."[15]

A passage that sums up these considerations is found in a late portion of The Book of Isaiah, probably written shortly before the fall of Babylon. It is a discussion of appropriate forms of worship, centered around the notion of fasting. The people are angry because they have fasted and God is not impressed. God responds that their fasting has only made them quarrel among themselves and oppress their workers. This is hardly the kind of fasting, or worship, that God wants. The appropriate alternative is then indicated:

> Is not this what I require of you as a fast:
> to loose the fetters of injustice,
> to untie the knots of the yoke,
> to snap every yoke and set free those who have been crushed?
> Is it not sharing your food with the hungry,
> taking the homeless poor into your home,
> clothing the naked when you meet them
> and never evading a duty to your kinsfolk?
> (Isa. 58:6–7)

4. Liberty to the Oppressed
(Luke 4:16–30)

If the story of the exodus is a paradigm for the Old Testament conviction that God takes sides, the story of Jesus' sermon in Nazareth (and what happened because of it) is a paradigm for the New Testament conviction that God brings liberty to the oppressed.

In the Lucan chronology, this is Jesus' first public appearance after the baptism-temptation experience which clarified his Messianic vocation. He returns to his hometown, and since it is Friday night he goes to the synagogue. He reads a passage from Isaiah (which we have quoted above) affirming that the gospel is directed to *the poor, the captives, the blind,* and *the oppressed.* It promises "release" from captivity and "liberty" for the oppressed, concluding with an announcement of the "jubilee year" that will involve a radical economic re-ordering. The message is cloaked with authority, for "the Spirit of the Lord" is upon the speaker and has anointed him to speak.

It is an astonishing passage. It is even more astonishing that after reading it Jesus has the audacity to say, "Today this scripture has been fulfilled in your hearing." He is announcing that the Messianic reign has already begun.

The initial reaction is one of approval. Faithful attenders at the synagogue have heard the Isaiah passage many times before, perhaps have even committed it to memory. They appreciate how well Jesus reads the words, they recall that he is Joseph's son and that they knew him when he was a boy.

But then the trouble begins. Jesus, not content to quit when he is ahead, points out that the gifts of God do not come automatically to those who attend the Temple. He cites two disturbing instances from the past: during a famine, help came to a woman from Sidon, a country far to the north, but not to the Israelites; and during the plague, healing came to Naaman, a Syrian, but not to the Israelites. And this is really too much! The initial approval of the worshipers turns to outrage. (Clarence Jordan translates their reaction, in his Cotton Patch version of the gospels, "When they heard that, the whole congregation blew a gasket!") The idea that the message is for worthless outsiders rather than us! The very notion that nonbelievers will be the recipients of God's favor and we will not!

And so the story literally becomes a cliff-hanger; they take Jesus out of the synagogue and up the very steep hill at the edge of Nazareth to throw him over the edge. (He escapes this time, but later on he meets death on another hill.)

Let us say for the people that their reaction was honest. They had every right to be outraged. They had been going to the Temple for years and now some kid from down the block is telling them that foreigners and outsiders may be the recipients of a divine visitation before they are.

It would be a healthy thing if we could be outraged as well, if we could hear the stridency and abrasiveness of this message as clearly as the villagers did, once their liturgical veneer had rubbed off. For what do we hear in this story that offends us? We hear that *(a)* the gospel message is initially addressed not to us but to the poor and oppressed, *(b)* their liberation makes things risky for us since the nonpoor cannot anticipate gentle responses from the poor once the latter are free, *(c)* being "religious" (or whatever is for us the equivalent of going to the synagogue) is no guarantee whatever that the future will fall out happily for us, and *(d)* God may look upon rank "outsiders' (Chilean peasants, perhaps, or Zimbabwe army officers —rough equivalents of the widow from Sidon or Naaman the Syrian) with more favor than upon us.

A message like that—who needs it? Over the cliff with him . . .

5. The Judgment of the Nations
(Matthew 25:31–46)

Jesus' story of the sheep and the goats is a familiar one that reinforces, sometimes in surprising ways, themes we have been examining.

One thing usually overlooked is that the judgment rendered is not against individuals but against nations: "Before him will be gathered *all the nations.*" The familiar obligations to feed the hungry, visit the sick, and clothe the naked are not merely requirements of private, individualistic ethics; they are demands made upon the *social* structures of which we are a part. It is our society that is being called to account. This is a terrifying prospect for a nation like ours which, as we have already noted, has 6 percent of the world's population and consumes 40 percent of the world's resources.

This social dimension of judgment is crucial, but it must not be used to let individuals off the hook. So for both nations and individuals the story tells us that the ultimate test, the criterion of final accountability in God's sight, is *not* Do you know the creed, do you pray, are you careful about Sabbath observance, do you mention God in your constitution and on your coins? but rather: *What did you do for those in need?* The test is not "knowing" but "doing," or rather, it is recognizing that the only true knowing comes by doing. Jeremiah 22 once again.

The story also underlines that it is *through the neighbor that God is known.* If in Jeremiah "to know God is to do justice," in Matthew "to love Christ is to do justice"—a Christ who is found in the face of the one in need. Gutiérrez comments on the passage:

> We find the Lord in our encounters with persons, especially the poor, marginated, and exploited ones. An act of love toward them is an act of love towards God. . . . Nevertheless, the neighbor is not an occasion, an instrument for becoming closer to God. We are dealing with a real love of people for their own sake and not "for the love of God."[16]

A further insight from the story is that the "righteous" do not know that they are righteous, nor do the "unrighteous" realize until the end that they have been found wanting. When told that they have been ministering to Christ while ministering to the needy, the only reaction of the first group is one of surprise: "When did *we* see you hungry . . . or thirsty . . . sick or in prison?" Preparing for ultimate accountability is not a matter of scoring points or "doing things for others" to gain merit or come closer to God. It is a matter of responding to need, of doing justice, of letting that concern be the center of life—both for the individual and for the nation—and then being content to accept surprises without counting on them.

Conversely, failing to respond to need, doing injustice, and not realizing the consequences of what has been done lead to another kind of surprise, finding oneself or one's nation held accountable in the sternest fashion possible, at the time that one had complacently been assuming that all was well.

A HERMENEUTIC OF ENGAGEMENT

We seem to have been reading a different book from our Third World friends. For us, the Bible has generally been a book supporting and strengthening our own way of life; for them, it is a book challenging accepted values and breathing the passion of revolutionary change. Describing the approach to the Bible of Ernst Bloch (a Marxist philosopher who has taken the Bible more seriously than most Christians), Jan Lochman comments:

> The uniqueness of the Bible lies in its revolutionary character. Of course, the Bible is not only a book of revolution. . . . There are in fact, different Bibles. There is the *biblia pauperum* (the Bible of the poor), the revolutionary book, but so also there is the Bible of the lords and priests; and these two are basically different. Now these different Bibles are interwoven with each other. . . . Bloch has laid down a hermeneutical principle which can be used by most of us: the later editors have generally tried to cover up or even explain away the original revolutionary message of their forebears.[17]

If it is even minimally true that later editors have tried to cover up or even explain away "the original revolutionary message of their forebears," it is massively true that later commentators and interpreters have done so. It should be a cause of wonder and shame that the Biblical message (which we briefly sampled in the previous section) could have been so "tamed" and defused of revolutionary power by later generations of Christians—up to and including ourselves.

What we have to learn from our Third World sisters and brothers is that the Bible is, indeed, in Ernst Bloch's phrase, the *biblia pauperum*, the Bible of the poor, the revolutionary book. If that is so, the poor and the oppressed will have an initial advantage over us in hearing and interpreting the Biblical message, *because their situation is closer to that of the Biblical writers than ours.* The revolutionary Bible was written out of situations of oppression, by the oppressed and for the oppressed. This suggests an important truth *for us* in Hugo Assmann's jarring phrase (used in the previous chapter) about "the epistemological privilege of the [struggling] poor." This does not mean neglecting the tools of Biblical scholarship that have been developed in centers of learning; anything that will help us toward a better understanding of the text is important. But it does mean that we must remain "suspicious" of conclusions about the Biblical message that defuse it of its revolutionary character.

So a hermeneutic of hope can never finally be a hermeneutic of detachment. It must be (in Beatriz Couch's phrase) "a hermeneutic of engagement." If the Biblical message embodies a bias toward the poor, that must be the bias contemporary readers of the Bible draw from it. If the Biblical message is that "to know God is to do justice," then the doing of justice must be the "engagement" by which contemporary readers of the Bible come to know God.

We can better illustrate a hermeneutic of engagement than describe it. The following is a true account in which only enough details have been altered to avoid casting suspicion on specific individuals. In a Central American country where there has been great persecution of church leaders, a number of priests have cast their lot with the poor, living in the slum area of a large city, working at whatever jobs (street-sweeping, house-painting) will pay for food and rent, and conducting informal Sunday "liturgies" at which the people comment on events of the week, and the priests relate those events to appropriate Biblical passages. One such exchange went like this:

PRIEST: Today is September 12. Does that date mean anything special to you?

RESPONSE: Three years ago yesterday Allende was killed in Chile and the Chileans lost their leader. Now they are suffering repression.

RESPONSE: Allende's death makes me think of the death of Mao.

RESPONSE: Their deaths make me think of the death of Martin Luther King.

PRIEST: Why do you think of the deaths of those three together?

RESPONSE: Because all three of them were concerned about oppressed peoples.

PRIEST: Doesn't the day mean anything but *death* to you?

RESPONSE: Well, today is also the Feast of the Holy Name of Mary. So this day also makes me think of her.

PRIEST: Is there any connection between Allende and Mao and Martin Luther King and Mary?

RESPONSE: I guess that would depend on whether Mary was concerned about oppressed peoples too.

PRIEST: Let me read part of Mary's song, the Magnificat, in the beginning of Luke's Gospel: "[God] has scattered the proud in the imagination of their hearts, he has put down the mighty from their thrones, and exalted those of low degree; he has filled the hungry with good things, and the rich he has sent empty away."

RESPONSE: Bravo! But, Father, that doesn't sound at all like the Mary we hear about in the cathedral. And the Mary in the "holy pictures" certainly doesn't look like a person who would talk that way.

PRIEST: Tell us about the Mary in the holy pictures.

RESPONSE *(displaying a picture):* Here she is. She is standing on a crescent moon. She is wearing a crown. She has rings on her fingers. She has a blue robe embroidered with gold.

PRIEST: That *does* sound like a different Mary from the Mary of the song! Do you think the picture has betrayed the Mary of the song?

RESPONSE: The Mary who said that God "has exalted those of low degree" would not have left all of her friends so she could stand on the moon.

CORPORATE RESPONSE: Take her off the moon!

RESPONSE: The Mary who said that God "has put down the mighty from their thrones" would not be wearing a crown.

CORPORATE RESPONSE: Take off her crown!

RESPONSE: The Mary who said that God "has sent the rich empty away" would not be wearing rings on her fingers.

CORPORATE RESPONSE: Take off her rings!

RESPONSE: The Mary who said that God has "filled the hungry with good things" would not have left people who were still hungry to wear a silk robe embroidered with gold.

CORPORATE RESPONSE: Take off her robe!

ANGUISHED RESPONSE: But, Father, this is not right! *(embar rassedly)* We're, we're doing a striptease of the Virgin.

PRIEST: Very well. If you don't like the way Mary looks in *this* picture, what do you think the Mary of the song would look like?

RESPONSE: The Mary of the song would not be standing on the moon. She would be standing in the dirt and dust where we stand.

RESPONSE: The Mary of the song would not be wearing a crown. She would have on an old hat like the rest of us, to keep the sun from causing her to faint.

RESPONSE: The Mary of the song would not be wearing jeweled rings on her fingers. She would have rough hands like ours.

RESPONSE: The Mary of the song would not be wearing a silk robe embroidered with gold. She would be wearing old clothes like the rest of us.

EMBARRASSED RESPONSE: Father, it may be awful to say this, but it sounds as though Mary would look just like me! My feet are dirty, my hat is old, my hands are rough, and my clothes are torn.

PRIEST: No, I don't think it is awful to say that. I think the Mary you have all described is more like the Mary of the Bible than the Mary we hear about in the cathedral and see in all the holy pictures.

RESPONSE: I think she'd be more at home here in the slum with us than in the cathedral or the General's Mansion.

RESPONSE: I think her message is more hopeful for us than for them. They are mighty and rich, but she tells them that God puts down the mighty from their thrones and sends the rich away empty.

RESPONSE: And we are at the bottom of the heap and very hungry, but she tells us that God exalts those of low degree and fills the hungry with good things.

PRIEST: Now let's see, how could we begin to help God bring those things to pass?

CHAPTER 4

Chords of Discord:
A Twelve-Tone Scale
of Sorts

(A Critique of Critiques:
Pros and Cons, Sharps and Flats)

> We must . . . try to sharpen the criticism in order to carry
> forward our dialogue.
>
> —*José Miguez-Bonino*

> Confrontations can shatter a dialogue, but they can also
> lead the participants out of a superficial friendliness into
> a deeper community.
>
> —*Jürgen Moltmann*

We have been engaged in an exposition of major themes of liberation
theology. Before we respond to such themes (a task that will occupy
us in Chapters 5 and 6), we need to confront criticisms that have
been leveled at this "theology in a new key." This will be the task
of the present chapter.

We are accustomed to musical scales that follow expected patterns, going up and down the white keys of the piano. We are also
accustomed to scales involving both white and black keys, but still
following predictable progressions of seven notes up or down the
keyboard. What we are *not* accustomed to are scales involving all
twelve notes (the seven white keys and the five black keys). Such a
scale is appropriately called a twelve-tone scale, and composers arbi-
trarily arrange such a scale *in any sequence they desire*. The only rule

imposed upon composers is that after constructing such a scale they must write their compositions in conformity with the rules of the musical logic of that new situation.

The present chapter resembles a twelve-tone scale in two respects. First, it deals with critiques of liberation theology in ways that may seem to have no more sequential logic than do the notes of a twelve-tone scale. The logic of this construction, to prepare the untrained, will be an attempt to progress from less significant to more significant critiques. Second, just as composers make an arbitrary arrangement of scales and notes, so the arrangement of critiques is arbitrary; other classifications are possible, provided they also follow the rules of logic their own order imposes.

I will try to be fair in assessing these critiques, but I cannot claim dispassionate neutrality. Too much is at stake in the lives (and deaths) of too many people for us to pretend that the pros and cons of liberation theology constitute a genteel parlor game. Since I believe that liberation theology provides a fresh clarification of the Christian gospel for our time and thereby greater possibilities for human justice, I have a partisan interest in seeking to remove all unnecessary roadblocks to its acceptance.

An Eightfold Sequence of Critiques

The arbitrary sequence of critiques is eightfold (not twelve—this is only a twelve-tone scale of sorts):

1. defensive critiques
2. total rejection critiques
3. oversimplified critiques
4. pseudo-issue critiques
5. reductionist critiques
6. methodological critiques
7. co-optation critiques
8. dialogical critiques

The first four do not seem particularly damaging (though they are unfortunately so widespread as to necessitate more than cursory rebuttal), whereas the last four raise substantive questions and merit serious attention that the present chapter can only begin to initiate.

1. Defensive Critiques

It is unfair to dismiss a point of view by imputing base motives to those who hold it. So we cannot dispose of specific critics of liberation theology merely by asserting that they feel threatened and therefore assume a defensive posture. Let us rather acknowledge that on a certain level this is true of *all* of us: we feel under attack and wish to defend ourselves. We feel excluded when told that "only the poor can do theology"; we feel insecure when we read that "the traditional theology of Europe and North America is bourgeois"; we feel indicted when we are described as "oppressors" who use theology to support the *status quo*. We want to insist that white, middle-class people can *also* do theology.

On a deeper level, we react not only with defensiveness but (as part of a widespread middle-class syndrome) with guilt. We are rendered uncomfortable by charges that we eat and theologize while others starve, or that our nation procures its wealth by exploiting poor nations. The trouble with the guilt-trip trap is that it is just that— a trap that immobilizes us, so that not only do we do nothing but become even guiltier because we are doing nothing.

Another defensive reaction is to reply, "You call us oppressors, but we are oppressed also just as you are." There is some legitimacy to the rejoinder that all people suffer certain forms of oppression, and we shall deal with it more fully under "co-optation critiques." For the moment, however, we must acknowledge significantly different degrees of oppression. It is one thing to be oppressed by tensions that drive us to eat or drink too much, and another thing to be oppressed by an economic system that deprives us of anything to eat or drink at all.

We can learn some positive things from our defensiveness in the face of liberation theology. For one thing, we *need* to be confronted with challenge in order to be jolted out of complacency. If middle-class values warp our theological perspective, we need to be reminded of that. If we are part of a system that benefits us by exploiting others, it is important to learn the truth about ourselves, even if its initial reception threatens to immobilize us.

It is also important to remember that *any* confrontation between the gospel and our human situation is threatening. In Kierkegaard's terms, only when we have gone through at least "the possibility of offense" can we claim to have encountered the true gospel. In *Training in Christianity,* he notes various ways in which the gospel message is an affront to us: we are offended, for example, by the notion that in assuming human form, God did so as a working-class Galilean peasant, who never made it through high school and was executed as a criminal while still a young man. (The use of Kierkegaard is important; my educated guess is that he would have been highly offended by liberation theology.) That something offends us is not, of course, a guarantee that it is true; but the mere fact of being offended is no assurance that the object of offense is false.

Finally, defensive critiques may tell us something about those engaging in the critique. To criticize liberation theology for Marxist leanings may be a way of trying to defend capitalism. To object to "the epistemological privilege of the poor" may be a way of insisting that affluence is perfectly respectable. Furthermore, certain criticisms of liberation theology merely cancel one another out. Segundo points out that César Aguiar characterizes Gustavo Gutiérrez as the leader of the "mass-oriented faction of liberation theology," while Ernesto Rosas accuses Gutiérrez of being "elitist."[1] One cannot have it both ways; we learn more about the critics than about the object of their criticism when confronted with such conflicting assessments.

2. Total Rejection Critiques

To be put on the defensive by the claims of liberation theology is at least a left-handed tribute; it implies that there is enough truth in the position to have struck close to home. But there are other critics who feel that the position is such a distortion and even a betrayal of the gospel that it must be rejected totally.

A forthright and therefore particularly helpful illustration of this position is the small book by Peter Wagner, *Latin American Theology.* Wagner's writing has stimulated Segundo to confront the issues raised, and in *The Liberation of Theology,* Segundo has isolated half a dozen points where he believes the issues are joined:[2]

First, Wagner believes that the function of the church is individual reconciliation, so that corporate groups' concerns are not part of the church's task. Second, among many tasks of the church, the priority always goes to the salvation of souls, so that any concern for social justice, while important, is secondary and derivative. Third, Christ's work is his activity within the church. To talk about the work of Christ in the world is a serious departure from the Bible. Fourth, "the unity of the church and membership in it is more important than any socio-economic-political option." Since Christians will always disagree in the latter area, church involvement in it will thus be divisive. Fifth, liberation theology fails to take seriously the dualism of the Bible, and attributes to natural or human causes what is actually the work of negative supernatural forces. Finally, liberation theology implies that salvation can be universally realized. Failure to be explicit on the eternal damnation of nonbelievers destroys the urgency of the gospel message.

Segundo asserts that he is not caricaturing Wagner's position (an assertion with which I concur), and he describes it as "the real merit" of Wagner's position that it spells out forthrightly the criticism that certain Roman Catholic ecclesiastical authorities have more covertly launched against liberation theology.[3]

It is not fair to let Wagner, whose personal commitment to evangelical Christianity is unassailable, stand as the only exemplar of the rejection of liberation theology. Similar rejections can be found elsewhere. The journal *Christianity Today* engages in frequent appraisals of liberation theology that cumulatively deny its Christian legitimacy. A single example, René de Visme Williamson's essay on "The Theology of Liberation," can communicate the flavor.[4] For Williamson, liberation theology is incompatible with Christianity. He feels, for example, that concern for "equality" is unbiblical. After token acknowledgment that certain human inequalities may be unfair, Williamson concludes: "Let us not forget that inequality of some kind is an inescapable fact of life. God did not endow us equally. There will never be complete equality on this earth and perhaps not in heaven either" (p. 12). A more Biblical approach, Williamson feels, will rely on Jesus' parable of the talents, which, he says, illustrates "the justice of inequality," and Jesus' own assertion that "the poor you have always with you." The inescapable conclusion in context is that liberation theology's concern to challenge inequities in modern society is contrary to Biblical Christianity.

Williamson repudiates the liberationist concerns for social change with the comment: "The advocacy of subversion and revolution runs counter to Romans 13, which instructs us to obey the powers that be" (p. 13). As any student of the New Testament will recognize, this is a highly arbitrary Biblical norm; Romans 13 must at least be considered in tandem with Revelation 13, which describes the state as "the beast." (Romans 13 was consistently used in Nazi Germany to justify allegiance to Hitler.) Williamson goes on to glorify Christians suffering under oppression and notes that slaves have been saved without legal emancipation. "The Church lives and thrives today under the Hammer and Sickle. Man has to realize that he is not God and *must learn to put up with some poverty, injustice and oppression*" (p. 13, italics added).

This joins the issues unambiguously. For Williamson there is no need to combat "poverty, injustice and oppression." We—or more precisely others—must simply learn to "put up" with such things. If that is indeed the Christian gospel, then liberation theology fails the test, for it is unambiguously committed to doing battle against such evils, especially as they victimize others.

Significant engagement between two such diverse interpretations of the Christian faith is almost impossible, whether the premises are the theological ones of Wagner or the ethical ones of Williamson. No genuine accommodation can be reached.

3. Oversimplified Critiques

Other criticisms of liberation theology are based on oversimplifications and distortions. Sometimes there are unqualified assertions that cannot withstand critical scrutiny. Williamson states, for example, that

> although the theologians of liberation acknowledge personal sin, they
> ascribe its existence to oppressive political and social structures; these
> *alone* produce and perpetuate it, they say;

and later on:

> It is significant that the doctrine of original sin plays *no part* in the
> thinking of the liberationists. That is why they do not recognize the
> ambivalence of resolution [*sic;* surely "revolution" is meant], which always
> engenders its Napoleons. (Pp. 7, 13, italics added)

The italicized words illustrate the problem. Liberation theologians
might be charged with overemphasizing the contribution of "oppressive political and social structures" to personal sin, but to charge that
they claim that personal sin is *exclusively* the product of such structures is simply an instance of polemical overkill. The same is true of
the charge that there is no recognition of original sin or "the ambivalence of revolution." Gutiérrez in particular stresses that revolution
must not be absolutized (cf. note 28, below).

On other occasions, sheer misinformation, not just overemphasis,
is communicated:

> As for the liberationists' espousal of secularization, it is enough to say that
> no doctrine that reads God out of life can rightfully be called Christian.
> . . . The idea that man is in full control and needs no supernatural help
> flouts reality. (P. 13)

One wonders how a person could read Gutiérrez, Segundo, Miguez-
Bonino, Dussel, and others and seriously assert that they "read God
out of human life." The one who "flouts reality" is the one who
makes such patently false assertions.

It is difficult to deal dispassionately with critiques of liberation
theology that include scorn for its proponents as well as oversimplifications. This attitude is exemplified by such widely syndicated "religious columnists" as Andrew Greeley and Lester Kinsolving, whose
irresponsibility belies their priestly calling and is undeserving of serious response. But it also occasionally overcomes the otherwise more
balanced judgments of such writers as Michael Novak, whose article
illustrates both characteristics.[5] Novak begins and ends on a note of

disdain, referring first to liberation theology as no more than "the newest theological fad," and ending with the comment, "We can expect liberation theology to become popular for while [*sic*, presumably "a while"]. Until a new and equally simple vision comes along." Such condescension demeans those Latin Americans who have put their lives on the line for a decade or more, convinced that the gospel demands their active opposition to repressive regimes. Similarly patronizing is the characterization of their liberation theology as "a weak imitation of Christianity. Most of it, ultimately, is the invention of white males from Eastern Europe. Most of it is cheap Marxism." Surely those who have had deep involvement in the Latin-American church are inadequately characterized as possessing a Christianity that is a "weak imitation" of the real thing, or of possessing scripts for discipleship in Latin America that were written in "Eastern Europe." And their Marxism, born out of engagement in the slums, is hardly "cheap."

Turning from *ad hominem* attack, Novak characterizes liberation theology as being "guilty of three heresies."

> First, it places far too much hope in history. Second, it places its hopes in a humanization and sanctification of the world, the flesh and the devil, not through grace but through politics. Third, it assumes that victims of oppression are innocent, good, the bearers of grace, rather than carriers of evils just as devastating as those of "oppressors."

Although there is some truth in these characterizations, they are too sweeping to carry persuasive weight. Is it placing "far too much hope in history" to work and act for the overthrow of structures of injustice? Is it wrong to hope for "a humanization and sanctification of the world," and to work politically toward that end, offering one's politics as a possible vehicle for grace? (Novak is theologically wrong to make "grace" and "politics" mutually exclusive, and substantively wrong to assert that theologians such as Miguez-Bonino, Gutiérrez, and Segundo disbelieve in grace as a vehicle of humanization and sanctification.)

Novak concludes that "liberation theology simplifies morality too much. It divides humans between 'good' and 'evil' so neatly that careful thinking is no longer necessary." When one has read Gutiérrez on the ambiguity of all utopian hopes, or Paulo Freire on the temptation of the oppressed to imitate oppressors, or Miguez-Bonino on the pervasiveness of sin in all levels of life, one realizes that "careful thinking" is also important for liberation theology's critics. It is appropriate for critics to level their guns at those of us in North America who, like the critics, theologize out of affluence and privilege. But it is another matter to dismiss those in situations of difficulty who struggle constantly to find the best ways to attack oppression.

A more sober though still oversimplified critique is found in David Tracy's *Blessed Rage for Order.* Tracy writes:

> [The] contemporary "political" theologians of *praxis*—of whom Jürgen Moltmann, Johannes Metz, Carl Braaten, Reubem Alves, Richard Shaull, Juan Segundo, Gustavo Gutiérrez and Dorothee Sölle appear most representative—seem, in most cases, to have transformed a neo-orthodox model for theology. Instead of challenging that model's basic adequacy, they have proposed new resources for actualizing the model in the present situation.[6]

In the midst of many penetrating insights, this characterization is too sweeping. It is not accurate to describe Alves, Shaull, Segundo, Gutiérrez, and Sölle as attempting to actualize a neo-orthodox theological model (whatever may be said for Moltmann, Metz, and Braaten). Furthermore, many Latin Americans have explicitly differentiated their position from the European "political theology" of Metz and Moltmann. It will not do to level criticism at Moltmann, as Tracy does (pp. 255–256), and assume that somehow Latin-American liberation theologians are tarred by the same brush, since (as we will see later) Moltmann has been a particular target of Miguez-Bonino, Gutiérrez, Assmann, and others. Tracy's criticism of Gutiérrez (p. 255) for challenging the notion of "development" but never challenging a major Christian doctrine is weakened by Gutiérrez's long distinction between salvation as quantitative and salvation as qualitative.[7] Finally, Tracy's hope that the more alert "revisionist theologians of *praxis* may also be able to resist the sirens calls of 'revolution' " (p. 249) implies a violence-prone type of liberation theology that (as our discussion below will try to show) the facts do not warrant. Because Tracy is so influential, one hopes that he will consider liberation theology more fully in subsequent writings.

4. Pseudo-Issue Critiques

The most frequent criticism of liberation theology is that it glorifies violence. This creates a "pseudo issue," not because violence is a pseudo issue (it is perhaps the major issue of our time), but because the centrality accorded it by the critics is utterly disproportionate to its place in liberation theology itself.

Williamson, for example, writes that "the concept of violence plays an important role in the theology of liberation," that while some theologians distinguish between violence by public authorities and counterviolence by private persons, "most of them do not bother" to do so, and that "in any case the liberationists hold that violence is necessary."[8] Such statements confuse rather than clarify. It is true that "violence plays an important role," but this is because *it is already a reality* in the societies where liberation theologians dwell, and there is no way that they could ignore it. It is *not* true that "most of them" do not bother to distinguish between the violence of the ongoing social structures and the possible use of "counterviolence" as a last resort against those structures. This distinction has been crucial from the time of the Medellín documents in 1968 (cf. paragraphs 15–19 in the Medellín document on "Peace"). Indeed, if one were to launch a critique, it would be that liberation theologians may have overplayed the distinction. Nor is it true that "in any case the liberationists hold that violence is necessary." This is particularly unfair, suggesting trigger-happy machine gunners in clerical collars rather than a sober conviction that, "if all else fails," a time may come when violence remains the lesser of two evils.

Hans Küng, in his widely read book *On Being a Christian*, has made a genuine effort to hear liberation theologians, and he avoids many of the oversimplifications we have been examining. But even he, affirming certain emphases of liberation theology, wants to make sure that we avoid "any theological glorification of violence."[9] The implication that liberation theologians engage in a "theological glorification of violence," or are tempted to do so, is a characterization that the facts will not warrant.

Peter Hodgson, in *New Birth of Freedom,* [10] discusses violence in relation to liberation themes and offers an alternative description of valid Christian strategy: "Conflict, struggle, the active and even revolutionary use of power, yes; but violence as a calculated policy or end in itself, no" (p. 320). Such alternatives are not descriptively fair, since no liberation theologian espouses violence as "an end in itself," nor does any other theologian. There is a particular irony in Hodgson's case, since shortly after having ruled out violence "as a calculated policy" he violates his own advice by saying, "Even when violence takes the form of killing, as in wars and revolutions, it cannot be denied that in the clearing created by violence new possibilities may sometimes emerge" (p. 321), adding that God can use revolutionary violence to create those new possibilities. Thus Hodgson comes perilously close to asserting for himself the right to a policy he denies to liberation theologians, and attributing to them a policy they do not hold.

The above are typical examples of the tendency to accuse liberation theologians of an espousal of violence. In reflecting on liberation theology's concern with the issue of violence, we can say a number of things:

1. The claim that attention to the issue renders liberation theology sub-Christian is unjustified. We have already noted that liberation theology *must* deal with violence since it is part and parcel of daily life in all oppressive situations. But to jump to the conclusion that such attention means that violence is being "glorified" or espoused as "an end in itself " is inaccurate.

2. If a theological position is invalidated because its concern for justice allows for violence as a last resort, almost all theological positions will be invalidated. One rarely hears the theology of Karl Barth invalidated for this reason, and yet in 1946—after the war was over —Barth wrote:

Violent solutions of conflicts in the political community—from police measures to law court decisions, from the armed rising against a regime that is no longer worthy of or equal to its task . . . to the defensive war against an external threat to the lawful state—must be approved, supported and if necessary even suggested by the Christian community—for how could it possibly contract out in such situations?[11]

Barth also says that violence is only a last resort, and that the church must be inventive in seeking other solutions—qualifications any liberation theologian would make—but he insists that the church can never stand for "peace at any price." Concern about violence is not something new in liberation theology, and the disproportionate attention focused on it by critics is itself disproportionate.

3. The reverse of the above point is that criticism of liberation theology because of its concern about violence can only be consistently urged by a pacifist, unless the critic is willing to invalidate all other theologies with a similar concern. A thinker like Gordon Zahn, whose pacifist credentials are unquestioned, is entitled to press the issue, and point out that any commitment to national liberation runs the danger of letting the ends sought determine too uncritically the choice of means.[12] This is a concern that any responsible person must heed.

4. It is also legitimate to question the human costs in the violence or terrorism of movements for social change, whether from the right or from the left. Peter Berger does this in *Pyramids of Sacrifice*, where he calls to account both the Brazilian model (development) and the Chinese model (revolution) for their willingness to sacrifice a whole generation, by terrorist tactics and the mass annihilation of political opposition, for the sake of a future that hopes to be free of such grim tactics.

The matter must not be oversimplified, however. An ethical dilemma remains with which Berger (at least in the writing under consideration) does not deal sufficiently, and which Denis Goulet has noted:

> Berger is correct in lamenting the high sacrifices demanded in the name of development and revolution; he is wrong in ignoring the equally high costs required by the stance of "keeping things as they are."[13]

Goulet goes on to point out that "there exist many protagonists of development, and even of revolution, whose commitment to avoiding elitist immolation of the masses is as unflinching as Berger's."

5. The basic issue is often lost in discussions such as the above critiques make necessary. It is frequently overlooked that violence does not first appear on the scene when somebody fires a gun or blows up a building. There is already the "structural violence" of a system that engages in silent genocide, the violence of injustice, starvation, and exploitation that destroys people just as effectively as guns or tanks. *The situation is already violent:* to ignore this fact is to condone structures that may be even more destructive than would be the "counterviolence" designed to create a new situation. In such a situation one might decide that the counterviolence would do more harm than the ongoing structural violence; or that the costs of the structural violence must be challenged by nonviolent means; or that one must create new structures to supplant the violent structures; or that the most one can do is keep hope alive in a distant future. Such options are all entertained by liberation theologians, together with a final option that when all else fails counterviolence might make the situation less unjust than it presently is.

The starting point is *the present reality of violence,* and the need to do something about it. For liberation theology the possible use of violence is not a first step but a last resort. The case of Camilo Torres (so often cited by critics as a typical exponent of violence) is instructive. Torres, as we recall from Chapter 2, was a Catholic priest in Colombia who tried every conceivable way of "working through the system" to change a repressive regime: he wrote, spoke, organized, marched, and voted. He gradually saw that those holding power remained unresponsive, and would resist violently any effort to bring about nonviolent change. After much thought and agony, and the gradual elimination of other alternatives, he concluded that *in that situation* no change could come by peaceful means, so he joined the guerrilla forces and was shortly thereafter killed in battle. His decision was a last resort, not a first step.

It is crucial to recognize the reality of violence within the unjust structures of contemporary society. How one deals with such violence is an issue no one can avoid. And little help is given by quick dismissals of those who live daily with such dilemmas and conclude that the use of counterviolence might one time become a moral necessity.[14]

5. Reductionist Critiques

Some critics of liberation theology claim that although it contains notes that ring with authenticity, the notes are selectively chosen and do not comprise a full scale: the total gospel has been "reduced" to ethics or politics or sociology or Marxism.

Much of the emphasis in liberation theology on ethics, politics, sociology, and Marxism is explained by the fact that other theologies have neglected those areas of concern and there is a vacuum to be filled. But this hardly justifies the charge that liberation theology is *nothing but* ethics, or that the church is only (as one critic puts it) "a recruitment office for the revolution." If we are to take liberation theologians at their word, they are not "reducing" the faith, but looking for ways to expand the faith so that it can speak to the situations where God has placed them:

> Our purpose is not to elaborate an ideology to justify postures already taken, nor to undertake a feverish search for security in the face of the radical challenges which confront the faith, nor to fashion a theology from which our political action is "deduced." *It is rather to let ourselves be judged by the Word of the Lord, to think through our faith, to strengthen our love, and to give reason for our hope from within a commitment which seeks to become more radical, total and efficacious.* It is to reconsider the great themes of the Christian life within this radically changed perspective and with regard to the very questions posed by this commitment.[15]

Miguez-Bonino similarly makes his theological position clear in the Preface to *Christians and Marxists,* and it is not a reductionist vision:

> This book is written from the point of view of a person who confesses Jesus Christ as his Lord and Saviour. This is his center of gravity and everything else is seen (in intention, at least) in relation to it. The reality and power of the Triune God, the witness of Holy Scriptures, the story of God's salvation are not seen as hypotheses to be proved, but as the foundation of life, action, understanding and hope.[16]

A distressing instance of the use of the reductionist charge has recently surfaced in Peru. A Salesian priest, Fr. Alejandro Cussianovich, recently published a book called *Desde los Pobres de la Tierra: Perspectivas de Vida Religiosa.* [17] In it a close connection is established between the Kingdom of God and the liberation of the poor of the earth:

> The Kingdom of God is revealed and concretized historically in the movement of all the poor, humiliated and despoiled who struggle for justice, freedom and love; this is the historical project of liberation of those who are accounted the scum of the earth.[18]

Cussianovich concludes that those in "religious life" (i.e., members of religious orders) must make "a total dedication to the poor in their struggle for justice." This is consistent with Catholic ascetic theology, particularly for those who take a vow of poverty, and Cussianovich argues that the traditional religious vows "lose their prophetic quality if they are not linked with the liberating process on behalf of oppressed people in Latin America."

Such conclusions have been held by his religious superiors in Rome to reduce the gospel to politics, and the book has been declared "heretical." The secular press in Peru has exploited the affair as another opportunity to discredit liberation theology, and has attacked Gutiérrez as "the father of heretics," since Cussianovich makes many references to him. One of Cussianovich's defenders, Ricardo Antoncich, S.J., notes that the ease with which ecclesiastical censors label the book "Marxist" suggests that most of the papal "social encyclicals" as well as the Magnificat should also be labeled Marxist, since they too challenge unjust social structures.[19]

The Marxist allegation is a frequent part of the reductionist critique. T. F. Torrance, a Scots Presbyterian theologian, accuses liberation theology of having "assimilated the prophetic passion of Jewish messianism, and the revolutionary nature and impetus of the Christian message, to Marxist ideology."[20] He overlooks the possibility that Marxism might be a useful tool of interpretation, assuming that it has become normative and swallowed up any distinctive Christian emphases. So liberation theologians are accused of adopting "a causal interpretation of human affairs and a materialist framework for all human ideals," and of believing in a utopia that "ultimately relies for its fulfillment on violence" (p. 10). Such "an alliance" with Marxism will "empty [the church's] message of its biblical and evangelical content." The exposition in previous chapters clearly establishes that such reductionism is unwarranted.

The reductionist critique often charges that liberation theology's *use of the Bible* is too selective, and that a small group of passages become normative for the rest. John Howard Yoder questions the emphasis on the exodus motif in liberation theology.[21] The exodus, he insists, is not the only Biblical image nor is it necessarily the central one, and the Bible's message is twisted when everything else is interpreted in its light. Yoder presses for more attention to other images, such as Bethel, and suggests that even the exodus story is not necessarily a helpful model for Christian engagement today, since it proposes walking away from the scene of trouble. Others ask whether the New Testament can be subsumed as fully into passages like Luke 4:16–30 (Jesus' sermon in Nazareth) and Matt. 25:31–46 (the story of the Last Judgment) as liberation theologians seem to imply. Does "to know God is to do justice" offer an adequate rendition of the *full* message of the Bible? Doesn't so much attention to the social dimension of the Biblical story eclipse the individual dimension?[22]

Dialogue about these concerns needs to continue. But we need to remember, as the dialogue proceeds, that *all* Christians read the Bible "selectively," and that the tendency to develop a working "canon within the canon" was not invented in Lima or Montevideo. It is universal. The Protestant Reformation was an exercise in reading the Bible from the vantage point of "justification by faith" or "salvation by grace alone"; pacifists interpret Scripture in the light of certain passages that become normative for interpreting other passages; the story of Jesus can be read from socialist, free enterprise, mystical, or "social gospel" perspectives. What is needed is not only a rigorous use of textual criticism to get as close as possible to the original meaning of the text but a continual exchange of exegetical conclusions, so that those who have warped the message can be called to account. The goal is not to have one bias win out, but to subject all biases to the closest approximation of the Scriptural bias we can corporately discern, recognizing that liberation theologians may be closer to the Biblical message than we are.

A third type of reductionist critique charges that liberation theology is *partisan,* insisting that its proponents "take sides," and thereby destroy the universality of the gospel's claim. The church, so the Chilean bishops argued in condemning Christians for Socialism, is called upon to minister to all, not just to the poor and oppressed.[23] Attempts to act in politically partisan fashion will jeopardize its inclusive fellowship.

Richard Neuhaus criticizes Gutiérrez along these lines, feeling that Gutiérrez overpoliticizes the gospel.[24] Acknowledging that the gospel has often been a captive of the right, Neuhaus accuses Gutiérrez of making it a captive of the left, and proposing "the Church as recruitment office for the revolution" (p. 45). Neuhaus feels "that [Gutiérrez] finally equates the Church's mission with the revolutionary struggle," the familiar reductionist charge (p. 45).

> *A Theology of Liberation* comes close to providing carte blanche legitimation for joining almost any allegedly revolutionary struggle to replace almost any allegedly repressive regime. . . . [It] comes very close to being an indiscriminate apotheosis of diverse revolutionary struggles. (Pp. 46, 47)

This charge of "partisanship" is based on the questionable assumption that one can be neutral. Liberation theologians vigorously challenge the validity of the assumption. To them the charge of "partisanship" is not polemical against some but descriptive of all. The question is never, *Shall* we take sides? but With whom are we *already* siding? and With whom *ought* we to be siding? Those who claim neutrality actually support those in power. Beatriz Couch puts the matter even more strongly:

> To think that we can be neutral in today's world is to believe that we can fail to be present, that we can afford the luxury of being simply absent, taking no sides, no options. We are all present one way or another in this historical moment and *we either contribute to the liberation of the oppressed of the world or we contribute to exploitation and injustice.*[25]

Gutiérrez has frequently commented that Latin Americans who seek a third way *(tercerismo)* between capitalism and socialism invariably end up on the side of the *status quo,* giving at least implicit

support to the oppressors rather than explicit support to the oppressed. So Neuhaus' conclusion, "One's impression is that Gutiérrez' vision is not that of the Church renewed but simply that of
the Church switching sides" (p. 48), is baffling at best, and mislead-
ing at worst. When the church has sided with the oppressors for
generations, "switching sides" may be the clearest sign possible of
"the Church renewed," leading to a fresh appropriation of the Biblical story and a revitalization of the Christian community.

6. Methodological Critiques

Segundo claims that the important contribution of liberation theology is a new methodology that makes possible "the liberation of
theology" from methods that have allowed it to accept outrageous
inequities complacently. Thus freed, we can articulate a "theology of
liberation" engaged in what Gutiérrez calls "a reconsideration of the
great themes of the Christian life."

The stress on methodology has elicited the criticism that liberation
theology is as methodologically bound to a particular sociocultural
perspective as the theologies it seeks to replace, and that it operates
so exclusively out of the context of the poor that the context shapes
the theology rather than the other way around. The charge that
liberation theology is too contextually conditioned deserves further
consideration.[26]

We need to remember that *all* theologies are contextually conditioned. Early Christians theologized in relation to questions raised in
Alexandria or Constantinople, and their statement of faith varied
depending on whose questions they were answering. The fact that
most of them were males, usually from the intelligentsia rather than
the working class, further conditioned their responses. When theological centers moved to Europe, the different context produced a
different theology: the structure of the Latin language meant that
abstractions tended to replace dynamic Hebraic forms, and an Aris-
totelian starting point conditioned the finished product. That theologians today work out of a particular context (the economic exploitation of the poor, for example) should not be surprising. It has always
been so.

Furthermore, the nature of Christian faith dictates that its theologies be contextually conditioned. There is no way a historical faith that has received embodiment in particular times and places could be expressed other than through the cultural contexts in which it developed. Otherwise it could not be communicated, and would ipso facto cease to be "historical." Jesus was not an abstract instance of "humankind," nor an eternal principle; he was a first-century Jew who lived in a small town and never traveled far from it, thought with his contemporaries that David wrote all the psalms, expected the imminent end of the world, spoke Aramaic, and got hungry. He was part and parcel of the context in which he lived, and can be understood in no other way.

The nature of Christian faith demands contextuality—one context speaking to another context and demanding a response. The attempt to deny this and create a "perennial theology" is doomed from the start, whether the attempt be that of St. Thomas, The Book of Concord, or the Westminster Standards.

So contextuality is not a unique problem for liberation theology but a description of all theology. If we notice, rather promptly, that liberation theology comes out of a particular cultural situation, the insight should help us, almost as promptly, to discern the same thing about our own theology.

A second methodological critique challenges the adequacy of the tools that are used and the way they are used: the sociological analysis is "shallow," the Marxist vocabulary is only superficially related to the true realities of the situation, terms like "oppressor" and "oppressed" are used imprecisely, sloganeering replaces serious analysis.

We have already posed the terms of rebuttal: Does the analysis descriptively illumine our contemporary situation or not? Many Third World Christians claim that it does, and as a result they seek to act responsibly on the basis of such analysis. It is not sufficient to dismiss their distinction between oppressor and oppressed as "facile," simply because its descriptive power is not initially self-evident to us. When Christians elsewhere have found it helpful, we must attempt to see the world through their eyes and be ready, if need be, to acknowledge the persuasive character of the new description and re-order our own world in the light of it. That we have not previously seen the world from the perspective of "class struggle" does not establish the superficiality of the concept; it may only establish that we have hitherto viewed the world superficially through privileged eyes from which a great deal of human pain has been hidden, and that we need help from those who see more clearly.

These insights are important as white males attempt to respond to black theology and feminist theology. White males are not enchanted to be called either "racists" or "male chauvinists," but one does not escape the charges by labeling them shallow or methodologically narrow. Simply to realize that *one is perceived* as a racist or male chauvinist may open one up to truths about one's self that had never previously been confronted.

The need is for widened theological dialogue, for there is conflict between various expressions of liberating theology. Black theologians, for example, tend to feel that Latin Americans stress economic oppression so much that they virtually ignore the racial component of oppression; to blacks, racism is as prevalent in socialist as in capitalist countries. Latin Americans respond that racist mentalities are enhanced by economic insecurity; this nourishes other insecurities and leads people to look for scapegoats who "deviate" from the norm. The conference on black theology, held in August 1977 in Atlanta, made clear that economic analysis was beginning to be taken more seriously by black theologians—an indication that the dialogue has proved fruitful. Similarly, North American feminist theologians charge (correctly) that South American liberation theologians have paid scant attention to the liberation of women; there have been subsequent contacts between the two groups so that the theme is beginning to appear on Third World agendas.

A related methodological criticism is that liberation theologians allow their theology to be molded by sociology rather than the other way around: utopian views of human progress are equated with the Biblical view of the Kingdom of God, and the resultant theology creates an expectation of social change that the facts do not warrant.[27] In this view, liberation theology is a "soft utopianism" that contradicts the Biblical view of human nature and history and takes insufficient account of "the moral ambiguity that characterizes all forms of social existence" (p. 170). Consequently, people and social systems are too neatly divided into "good" and "bad," nations into "capitalist" and "socialist," and so on. Since these moralistic dichotomies are not descriptively true, the argument continues, they become strategically useless and even counterproductive.

A theology engaging in such oversimplification deserves to be called to account. But exponents such as Gutiérrez and Freire avoid this trap. Gutiérrez sees the danger of simplistic versions of the truth and is aware of the ambiguity of all historical achievements, and warns against political liberation

> being translated into any kind of Christian ideology or political action or [into] a politico-religious mechanism. Christian hope opens us, in an attitude of spiritual childhood, to the gift of the future promised by God. *It keeps us from any confusion of the Kingdom with any one historical stage, from any idolatry toward unavoidable ambiguous achievement, from any absolutizing of revolution.*[28]

It is a basic theme of Paulo Freire that

> the oppressed must not, in seeking to regain their humanity (which is a way to create it), become in turn oppressors but rather restorers of the humanity of both.[29]

A different sort of methodological critique challenges liberation theology not for being too avant-garde but for being too tied to the methodologies of the past. This new note is sounded by Alfredo Fierro, a Spanish theologian, in *The Militant Gospel.*

Fierro calls his own viewpoint a "historico-materialistic theology," dependent upon "the Marxist hypothesis of historical material-ism,"[30] which informs the historical and methodological critique of "political theology" he attempts. He wants to work out a "theology," which differs from a confession of faith or a profession of hope. While the latter may be testimony, they are not "theology." So Fierro distinguishes between "a theology in the strict sense" (talk about God) and "a theological ethics" (statements about moral doctrine). On these terms, liberation theology does not qualify as "theology in the strict sense"; it is rhetorical theology, telling us about the convictions of the believer, but providing no basis for that belief and supplying no cognitive content: "Such notions as brotherhood, liberation, communion, love and conversion are not theoretical or cognitive concepts, strictly speaking" (p. 316). Fierro believes, in other words, that liberation theologians confuse two kinds of language, theological language ("second-state critical reflection") and what he calls theologal language ("precritical expression of the faith"). He develops this technical distinction as follows:

> *Theologal language* has a proper place when and insofar as it remains fully aware of what it itself really is: i.e., direct, spontaneous, procritical expression of the faith. But when it passes itself off as *theology in the strict sense,* as second-stage critical reflection on the faith, then it is expropriating a place to which it has no right. . . . If we want to keep calling it theology, then we should call it poetic theology, or homiletic theology, or rhetorical theology; we should not call it critical theology. (P. 318, italics added)

This means that the language of liberation theology is hopelessly muddled. Its discussions of revolution, rapid social change, and so forth, "do not rise above the level of poetic or rhetorical theology" (p. 323).

Such a distinction allows Fierro to characterize Gutiérrez's *A Theology of Liberation* as "an excellent book as witness and testimonial," but "not always theology in the strict sense" (p. 324). He asserts that Gutiérrez operates within the realm of "dogmatic theology" (statements that assume truth of the Catholic faith), rather than "fundamental theology" (statements whose truth one attempts to validate by argument). And Fierro's ultimate criticism—a completely arbitrary one—is that liberation theology should be the latter rather than the former. This enables him to make the otherwise astonishing statement about Gutiérrez, "We are hearing a Christian, not a theologian, speaking" (p. 328), as though the terms were mutually exclusive. Gutiérrez is scored not for having written the book he wrote, but for not having written the book Fierro thinks he should have written. Fierro's argument reduces to the unproved but firmly stated assertion that liberation theology must be "fundamental theology," and that since it is only "dogmatic theology" it fails to meet the criterion the critic has personally established for it.

Fierro feels that Gutiérrez is limited to pushing for a "restoration of the sacred" rather than an acceptance of the secular. His theology is thus "full of vestiges and reminiscences" (p. 342), to be linked (astonishingly) with Teilhard de Chardin, beyond whom, Fierro claims, Gutiérrez advances not a single step. Gutiérrez combines "social progressivism with theological conservatism" (p. 344), whereas Fierro believes we must "adopt Marxism as our hypothesis and then go on to consider what sort of theology is possible on that basis" (p. 370). This helps to clarify a basic distinction between the two. For Fierro, Marxism is an intellectual hypothesis to be tested. He is still responding to the question of the nonbeliever, rather than responding to the situation of the nonperson. His is a theology of the intellect rather than a theology of engagement.

This brief discussion of Fierro is important not only as an example of two mutually exclusive methodologies but also as a reminder that not all critiques of liberation theology come from the right. Whereas most critiques fear "too much Marxist methodology," Fierro, working from the intellectual left, is critical because he feels there is too little.

7. Co-optation Critiques

The late Huey Long is credited with having said, "Someday we'll have fascism in the United States, only we won't call it that, we'll call it democracy." That is a splendid example of co-optation: take something that threatens you (like democracy) and claim it as your own by transforming it into its opposite. The theological counterpart for Huey Long's affirmation would be, "Someday we'll have an unthreatening theology in the church, only we won't call it that, we'll call it liberation theology."

Third World theologians are understandably nervous as they observe North Americans beginning to use the vocabulary of liberation theology (and even writing books about "theology in a new key"). Hugo Assmann's warning is salutary:

Perhaps the first important contribution Christians can make to the process of liberation is not to add to the process of diluting the revolutionary implications that circumstances have dictated it should contain.[31]

The "revolutionary implications" about which Assmann speaks can be avoided by the process of co-optation insisting, for example, that we use liberation in the "full meaning" of the term, talking about the liberation of the soul, or liberation from guilt, as well as physical liberation; talking about spiritual liberation or inner liberation as well as political liberation. The resulting construction can be called *authentic* liberation theology.

There is no doubt that such concerns are a part of the gospel, and we have already seen that liberation theologians are not blind to them. But the critique under examination is usually employed to suggest that if we first take care of inner, spiritual liberation—the "basic" liberation, it might be called—the outer, political, and economic liberation will take care of itself: changed individuals will produce a changed society. This ignores a stubborn fact that liberation theologians emphasize: individual sins get lodged in corporate structures in ways that virtually endow socialized forms of evil with a life of their own. It ignores a further stubborn fact that changed individuals do not necessarily produce a changed society; they may fight with greater zeal than ever to see that society as they know and love it remains unchanged.

Another mode of co-optation is to claim that all of us are in the same boat as those crying for liberation from oppression. "We are *all* oppressed," this argument goes, "if not by dictators then by middle-class mores; if not by multinationals starving us then by the multinationals hounding us to show a bigger profit; if not by low incomes then by high taxes."

There is provisional truth in the argument and we will build on it in the next chapter. But the argument must not be employed too quickly *(a)* to get us off the hook for the degree to which we do benefit from oppressive structures and are complicit in the oppression they work on others, or *(b)* to offer what can only appear to be cheap alliances to those who have every reason to distrust us, or *(c)* to gloss over the gulf that remains between our own aspirations for liberation and the aspirations of "the wretched of the earth."

Honest readers will recognize their own employment of the co-optation techniques described above, along with others so subtle as to escape detection. But the temptation is real not only in North America but in South America as well, and it will be instructive to observe how a Roman Catholic theologian, Bishop Lopez Trujillo, "spiritualizes" the notion of liberation, so that all offense and challenge are removed from it. To get the full flavor of the debate, we will include responses by a proponent of liberation theology, Fr. Roberto Oliveros, S.J.[32]

Lopez accepts *dependency* as a description of Third World reality but balks at accepting any given *theory of dependency*. When Gutiérrez states that the underdevelopment of the poor nations is caused by the overdevelopment of capitalist nations, Lopez demurs, questioning whether such a conclusion is "scientific," and concluding that Gutiérrez is excessively dependent on an "economic" interpretation that overemphasizes the structures of production. Oliveros counters that one *must* offer interpretations and that to press an economic one does not rule out others, since the issue is clearly political as well. Lopez's rejection of such interpretations simply implies his acceptance of some other interpretation.

Lopez rejects the use of Marxist methodology, particularly when it is projected globally. Oliveros replies that Lopez need not fear that the use of Marxist analysis means undermining the faith. What it does mean is a commitment to transform society on behalf of the poor and a rejection of the bourgeois vision of God.

While Lopez accepts the reality of conflict, he rejects the notion of "class struggle," preferring to speak of "the struggle for justice." Oliveros responds, "It is natural that one who does not accept the social diagnosis offered by a theory of dependence will not want to take the medicine that goes along with it" (p. 322). All Christians should be committed to "the struggle for justice," but if this is to be more than words, it must involve commitment with the poor in revolutionary praxis, which means taking sides, which means one class against another. Lopez, however, fears that "class struggle" will lead to violence, which both the gospel and natural law forbid. Oliveros replies that Lopez's analysis fails to go to the root of the problem: the "institutional violence" of the *status quo* and the "counterviolence" that may be needed to eradicate the social injustice of the *status quo,* cannot be equated so easily. "Spiritualizing" has taken over and denied that theology need have a political or ideological character.

Lopez worries that liberation theology will serve class interests and become an ideology. Oliveros replies that theology is always expressed in human categories that are permeated by ideology. Lopez's own position has an ideological or class taint, since he uses Aquinas' dependence on "natural law" to justify private property. Even the attempt to "spiritualize" theology is dependent on an ideology that meshes neatly with the *status quo:* how else can one describe the defense of private property in a capitalist culture? A further proof of this hidden ideology is the fact that Lopez's references to capitalism are always in the context of its "reformability," whereas references to Marxism always assume that it is static. So Lopez's own theology is an ideological vehicle for the furtherance of certain class interests.

In his critique of a politicized church, Lopez insists that Paul stayed free of divisive politics and stressed "brotherhood." Oliveros calls this hollow advice in Latin America. How are the masses able to be "Christian brothers" with the unscrupulous rulers in Brazil or the exploiters in the slums? How can one share the Eucharist on Sunday with people who spend the other six days of the week torturing political prisoners?

Lopez's "spiritualizing" extends to his treatment of the poor. Oliveros responds that Biblical passages about the poor having their treasure in heaven represent only one aspect of the Biblical message, and that it is false to make them normative for the whole. Lopez appears to miss the Bible's outrage at poverty; in his "Lutheran dualism" the sociopolitical realm is not an object of salvation. When this view of poverty is accepted, any struggle for liberation disappears, the solidarity of Christ with the poor is lost, religion becomes "the opiate of the people," and oligarchies can breathe freely again.

The theme of reconciliation is also "spiritualized." Lopez insists that the gospel message is not violent conflict or class struggle, but reconciliation. There is no hope for solutions by conflict; peace is a gift; unity is grace. Oliveros responds that while unity is a grace, none of this can go bail for human responsibility: "I have never seen it rain tractors," he writes, "but I have seen men in the steel plants and factories working to get them." Reconciliation doesn't happen in the realm of good intentions but in better or worse social systems.

In practical terms, Oliveros concludes, such consistent "spiritualization" coincides with the interests of the powerful rulers. Consequently, they all support this version of theology and brand themselves "liberators." Thus is the co-opter himself co-opted.

8. Dialogical Critiques

Many of the above critiques are critiques "at a distance"; the protagonists fail to encounter one another. Creative critique involves a genuine exchange—a dialogue—in which adherents of different positions challenge one another and are influenced by what transpires.

We are fortunate that such a dialogue is now in process. Miguez-Bonino began it in *Doing Theology in a Revolutionary Situation,* raising questions about the theology of Jürgen Moltmann; Moltmann responded in an "open letter," raising questions about liberation theology. This in turn has sparked numerous Latin-American responses, shortly to be published, and Moltmann traveled extensively in Latin America in the fall of 1977 to continue the exchange.[33] Let us eavesdrop on the initial dialogue.

Miguez-Bonino describes Moltmann as "the theologian to whom the theology of liberation is most indebted and with whom it shows the clearest affinity" (p. 144). He outlines important contributions from Moltmann's *Theology of Hope* and *The Crucified God,* but then observes that Moltmann misses the real challenge of Latin-American theology.

His first criticism is that Moltmann's social analysis remains abstract, describing "the demonic circles of death," and so on, "without giving a coherent socio-analytic account of this manifold oppression"

(p. 147). Theology must have "a coherent and all-embracing method of sociopolitical analysis. Moltmann does not seem to be conscious of this need" (p. 147).

More serious is Moltmann's failure to give a concrete content to "identification with the oppressed" (p. 148). Miguez-Bonino finds a contradiction within Moltmann's statement that "the crucified God is really a God without a country and without class. But he is not an a-political God; he is the God of the poor, of the oppressed, of the humiliated" (*The Crucified God*, p. 305). Miguez-Bonino insists that Moltmann cannot have it both ways:

> The poor, the oppressed, the humiliated *are a class* and *live in countries.* Is it really theologically responsible to leave these two sentences hanging without trying to work out their relation? Are we really for the poor and oppressed if we fail to see them as a class, as members of oppressed societies?[34]

Moltmann, Miguez-Bonino continues, draws back at the crucial point, suggesting a "critical function" for theologians which puts them "above right and left, ideologically neutral, independent of a structural analysis of reality," in order "to avoid sacralizing a particular ideology or power structure" (p. 149). While Miguez-Bonino agrees that we must not sacralize any ideology, since "there is no *divine* politics or economics . . . , this means that we must resolutely use the best *human* politics and economics at our disposal" (p. 149).

Thirdly, Miguez-Bonino calls on Europeans to desacralize their conception of "critical freedom." This is an expression of one particular ideology, the "liberal social-democratic project which progressive European theologians seem to cherish particularly." But it should not be presented as though it were "the critical freedom of the gospel"; it is simply the political option Europeans have made, just as others may opt for a Marxist analysis.

Moltmann's "open letter" is less a response to Miguez-Bonino's charges than it is an attempt to "clarify what we [Europeans] find dissatisfying in you [liberation theologians] and what we actually are expecting from you" (p. 57). He too (in good theological fashion) makes three points:

Moltmann first chides Latin-American theologians for their seeming ambivalence. The theology of liberation has a right to be indigenous, breaking loose from European chains, but this should not lead to provincialism in a time when we need a world theology. He then notes that African theology is contributing new insights along with Japanese theology and North American black theology. But Latin-American theology is still borrowing from Europe. What is the point of criticisms of European theology that are immediately followed by an appropriation of the very themes criticized?

Secondly, Moltmann challenges "the use of Marxism by Latin American theologians." There is not yet a Latin-American understanding of socialism. Moltmann claims to hear "declamations of seminar-Marxism as a world view," rather than an incisive Marxist analysis of Latin-American realities.

> The true radical change that is necessary is still ahead of both the "political theologians" in the European context and the "liberation theologians" in the Latin American context. In my opinion they can enter in a thoroughly mutual way into this change, namely a radical turn toward the people.[35]

This comment has something of an *ad nominem* flavor, since the Latin-American theologians discovered liberation theology by making "a radical turn toward the people." It was just such a turn that led to encounters with socialism as a serious option for Latin-American Christians.

Finally, Moltmann suggests that the real difference between European and Latin-American theologies lies in their "assessment of the various historical situations." Latin-American theologians fail to distinguish between the *necessity* and the *possibility* of a socialist revolution. The necessity of such a revolution is indisputable, but the possibility is far from being within reach. His indictment includes two stern images and a direct charge. Since intellectual revolutionary sparks cannot now ignite among the people, "the sparks then become sectarian candles around which elite circles gather ceremoniously in order to confirm themselves." Again, long trains frequently wait for locomotives to lead them to their destinations. But sometimes "the locomotive departs so quickly that the couplings are torn apart and the train remains motionless on the track." Locomotives then have to go back and get recoupled. Finally, "To say it without images, it seems more important to maintain a connection with the people than to travel alone into the paradise of the future. It is more important to live and work in and with people than to relish the classless society in the correct theories" (p. 61).

These are blunt statements, implying that Latin-American theologians as well as Europeans are elitists living in a world of intellectual theory, rather than identifying with the people, preferring correct theories to human identification. More helpful are Moltmann's concluding comments, offering his version of a liberating possibility for Europe through "democratic socialism."

A number of Latin-American theologians have prepared responses to Moltmann's letter, which will be published in a single volume. Gutiérrez's chapter has already appeared in Spanish, in which he argues that two different theologies are confronting one another: a theology in the "modern spirit," and a theology in a "world of oppression." There is a necessary rupture between them.[36] Other Latin-American theologians have commented that they see Moltmann caught in a "European liberal syndrome," advanced in relation to his own situation, but not on the cutting edge of liberation for oppressed people. They fear that his plea for a world theology will turn out to be an imposed "western" theology. Such a position basically accepts the present socioeconomic order, engages in "reformism from within," and seeks to move by "gradualism" to a more just social order. This is a luxury Latin Americans can no longer afford. They feel that Moltmann does not take praxis seriously enough, and that he is still engaged in intellectualizing. The issue for them is not new themes for reflection, but a new way of doing theology out of the slums rather than out of the universities. They continue to fear a theology that seems capable of remaining above the struggle.[37]

Each rereading of the Miguez-Bonino and Moltmann exchange leaves one less satisfied that the issues have been fully joined by Moltmann's response, though his forthrightness is impressive. But it is clear that such direct give-and-take is the appropriate model for the future. We can anticipate increasing help as the protagonists pursue the exchange face-to-face. In such encounters it will be increasingly difficult to talk past one another.

FROM CRITIQUES TO CREATIVE APPROPRIATION

We have now examined a substantial number of critiques of liberation theology. I do not feel that either individually or cumulatively they inflict mortal blows. It is therefore important to ask in what ways and to what degree we can appropriate, for our situation, the insights of a theology that has developed in another situation. If liberation theology speaks a true word for today, we must now ask what is its true word for us.

CHAPTER 5

"How Shall We Sing the Lord's Song in a Strange Land?": Discovering the Word of God for Us

(What Can We Learn from Elsewhere for Our Situation?)

> "How do you sing to God in a strange land?" the Psalm-ist asked in exile. Without "songs" to God, without celebrations of his liberating love, there is no Christian life. But—how do you sing to God in a land alien to his love, in a continent of oppression and repression? . . . This leads to an alliance with the world's poor, towards a new type of universality.
>
> —Gustavo Gutiérrez (the fuller context of the quotation at the head of Chapter 1)

The question of the forlorn writer of Psalm 137 (from which our chapter title is taken) suggests a situation different from our own. He or she was in exile, far from home in a land that was indeed "strange," and hardly receptive to "the Lord's song." We, however, are not in exile but at home, in a land that is about as close to "the Lord's" as anywhere we can imagine. Consequently, we may be tempted to reverse the query so that it goes, "How shall we sing a strange song in the Lord's land?"

But temptations to improve on Scripture are dubious at best, and we will assume in this chapter that the psalmist describes our own plight as well. The assumption is based on two things: (1) that the emphases of liberation théology are at least approximations of "the Lord's song" rather than aberrations of it, through which God is communicating to us as well as to Third World peoples, and (2) that this makes our present dwelling place a "strange land" (even though our geographical situation is unchanged), since we now have to think and act in ways that are alien to those around us, challenging what we have heretofore not only taken for granted but even held dear. From this perspective our land is indeed "strange," a place where profits are more important than prophets, where a few with great power make decisions for everyone else, where competition is a blessed word and cooperation is a weak word, and where most of our churches implicitly or explicitly support a political-economic exegesis of the Biblical promise that "the right shall prevail." How can we sing "the Lord's song" in this "strange land"?

REHEARING "THE LORD'S SONG"— A THREAT AND A CHALLENGE

It is obvious that to hear something involves a willingness to listen. It is less obvious, but more important, that we may not like what we hear; the new song may be such a threat or such a challenge, that we want to stifle it.

The Lord's song is clearly a *threat*. It is a threat to our personhood, suggesting that we are on the wrong side of the oppressor-oppressed dialectic; it is a threat to our faith, suggesting that we co-opt faith to allow us to side with the privileged rather than the needy; it is a threat to our nationhood, suggesting that we use our power for exploitive rather than creative purposes; and it is a threat to our will to change, suggesting that the price of change is more than we are willing to put on the line.

For many, the last point is the heart of the problem. Many of the structures of society that benefit us are structures that destroy others. Their backs and lives are broken producing the food we eat and the goods we purchase. They will never be able to stand as long as our feet are on their necks. Their exploitation seems to be necessary for our comfort. And unless we are callously insensitive, we cannot help being threatened by that discovery. We would like to change the world so that such conditions do not continue and we are further threatened when most of the things we are prepared to "do" are looked upon as cheap palliatives or trivial evasions of the real problem. Our concepts of "help," "charity," and "doing good" are interpreted as ways to salve our consciences without changing our lives. We attack the symptoms rather than the causes. This makes us feel better but *nothing has changed.*

It is the insistent call for radical change ("radical" in the sense of going to the *radix,* or root, of things) that is most threatening. It is one thing to affirm intellectually that if an economic system based on competition only grinds down and destroys, then the system must go, since it is not enough to have those on top grind with a smile on their faces instead of a sneer, or give an occasional charitable loaf of bread to those to whom they deny wages sufficient to buy loaves themselves. And yet, the argument that "the system must go" is a genuine threat, because with the disappearance of the system would go our securities, our status, our luxuries, possibly our necessities, perhaps even our lives.[1]

What would it take to move from threat to *challenge*— a challenge to change in spite of the risks? Here are a few ingredients that might help:

1. *A sense of frustration*— a recognition that we haven't got it all put together and that since there are still a lot of missing pieces maybe there is some point in listening to others. This could also be described, a little more profoundly, as:

2. *A sense of humility*— a recognition that the trouble may not be missing pieces, but our use of the wrong pieces—pieces from a capitalistic jigsaw puzzle to create the picture of a cooperative society, pieces from an individualistic Christianity to create concern for social justice. If it is hard to say "We're incomplete," it is still harder to say "We're wrong," but that makes it easier to listen to alternatives, even though they will confront us with:

3. *A sense of risk*— a recognition that listening to other alternatives is double-edged: on the one hand, risk that the new voices might

be *wrong*, leaving us in the situation of having been fooled twice; on the other hand, risk that the new voices might be *right*, leaving us in the situation of having to abandon many things we had previously assumed were secure, and beginning to look at the world and ourselves in new and unfamiliar and therefore risky ways. The risk of *having to change* is the biggest of all. An ability to handle it usually depends on:

4. *A sense of trust*— a recognition that the new voices make enough sense so that we are willing to trust that they do sing more than their own song and are mouthpieces for "the Lord's song," so that their melodies, however strident at first, can contribute to the reconstruction of ours. Since it is hard to trust the accuracy of individual judgments, we will be helped by:

5. *A sense of community*— a recognition that we are not called upon to do this in solitude but in company with others, with whom we can mutually check our decisions.

All of this is leading us toward a question. It is important that it be the right question. The question is *not*, How do we *transfer* liberation theology from South America to North America? as though it were simply a matter of repeating in and for our situation insights that were formulated in and for another situation. We are not to import other theologies wholesale, as though Gutiérrez were the new Aquinas, or Miguez-Bonino the new Wesley; nor are we to lift categories of social analysis uncritically from either Europe or Uruguay. The question is rather, As we observe how Latin Americans try to be faithful to the gospel in *their* situation, what does their experience tell us about how to be faithful to the gospel in *our* situation? *We are not to edit a North American edition of Latin-American theology but to create a new version of North American theology.*

RESINGING OUR OWN SONG— A MORE AMPLE ORCHESTRATION

We have already suggested that our understanding of the Bible can be altered as we confront other understandings of the Bible originating in situations different from ours.

The same thing is true of our understanding of our own story, of the singing of our own song.[2] We usually reflect upon our own stories from narrow perspectives that enfeeble our ability to relate them to the parallel stories of others. To the degree, however, that we can see them in wider contexts, we can increase our awareness of what this new perspective demands of us.

Let me illustrate this in personal terms.[3] For a significant portion of my own life I saw my story largely as a middle-class, white Anglo-Saxon Protestant male, born and reared in the United States—a vintage WASP. My perspectives were formed by the fact that I was a child of the manse, grew up in largely suburban surroundings, went to predominantly white public schools, attended an upper-middle-class (and exclusively male) college and a "liberal" interdenominational Protestant seminary—all on the Eastern seaboard. I was part of a majority, comfortable in the mores and patterns I unconsciously absorbed from that ethos. To be sure, Catholics, blacks, Jews, and members of ethnic minorities had a presence in my world, but it was usually a token presence.

The story of who I was, while adequate for survival in such a world, turned out to be far from adequate for the wider world into which I gradually went—a world by no means an extension of the one in which I had lived. Gradual conscientization was furnished by World War II, seeing Nagasaki after the bomb, participation in a Freedom Ride, various acts of civil disobedience in response to racism and Vietnam resulting in brief spells in a variety of jails, and other events that shattered my comfortable world.

What resulted was a recognition of the limited perspective of my own story, and a recognition that I must tell it differently. I now have to see my story and indeed the whole American story in relation to the *black story.* I can't do that fully, but I have to try. It is not only a different story from the one I learned in high school, but it is a judgment upon almost every interpretive comment that was in the history books. I have had to learn that "the land of the free and the home of the brave" is not "free" for black people, and that the reason it is not has something to do with white people who are not "brave" enough to confront the racial injustice embedded in the whole American way of life.

It was not until I moved to the West Coast that I had to confront the clash between my story and *the Native American story,* and internalize that what had previously been the noble story of "the white man's expansion of the West" was in reality the ignoble story of the white man's expulsion and near extinction of the red man (and woman and child), using techniques perfected by God-fearing Christians in the Massachusetts Bay Colony. It was a chillingly monotonous experience to drive west the summer of our move and discover that the Indian "reservations" always turned out to be the worst land.

The experience is similar when my male-oriented story confronts *the rising consciousness of women* that in the retelling of their stories, a major component is always the discovery of the systematic domination and putdown to which they have been subjected by men. That this may not always have been consciously contrived by me or my male compatriots (though it often has been) only deepens the hurt for both men and women when the discovery is made.

Such insights, it should be noted, came not out of my solitary reflecting on the meaning of my own story, but out of the impingement of other stories upon it.[4]

A further example is necessary. My American story has to be retold in the light of *the international story,* for my story, both as an individual and as citizen of a nation, has had an impact on other individuals and other nations. I was always told that this impact had been beneficent. It has been part of my recent "conscienticizing" to hear my American story told by Vietnamese and Chileans—and "beneficent" is hardly the word they use to describe our collective impact on them. Simply the sheer magnitude of the impact is crucial, whatever its quotient of beneficence or malevolence. Juan Luis Segundo makes the point in a speech given in the United States a number of years ago.[5] Segundo accepts the fact that the immediate outlook for Latin America is one of "poverty, instability, and tyranny." The extinguishing of significant hope for real change in Latin America means that "there is going to be neither evolution or revolution. All we can do is—hang on." He asks North Americans to realize that because of the economic dependency of Latin America on North America, decisions about the future of *Latin* Americans will be made by *North* Americans. This is not hopeful, since North American decisions will not be made to benefit Latin-American lives but to benefit North American profits.

Could this change? Segundo responds that raising the question demonstrates his hope for an affirmative answer, though he realizes that the demand for such change presents "one of the most arduous challenges ever presented to any people."

"In any case," he concludes, "the reply to the question 'How long will we have to hang on?' can only be this: 'Until this hope becomes a reality,' " i.e., until there is a basic change in North American attitudes.

Segundo's speech has haunted me for years, because it shows with devastating clarity how my story affects other stories. What I am doing with my life, and what we North Americans are doing with our lives, affects not only our own future but the future of our sisters and brothers in Latin America.

To many, such a conclusion approaches the nature of a truism; if that is so, it is a "truism" only for *us*. It is a truth of life and death for the others, because the way we go on telling our story will determine whether they are left with any story to tell at all.

Rewriting Our Christian Song— Attention to Neglected Themes

The same interrelationship applies to stories from the past. We have already examined how we are forced to hear Scripture in a new way when we let liberation theologians be our hermeneutical guides. But this is not the end of the process. There is a history of two millennia in which Christians not only have reflected on the Biblical materials but have fashioned theologies out of them and developed institutions based on them. It is hard to read theological or church history in charitable terms from a liberation perspective, so frequently have the theologies provided justification for the *status quo* and the churches provided spiritual homes for the oppressors.

One may argue that this will always be so and that the sooner one breaks with such tradition the better. Or one may argue (as we shall now attempt to do) that there is a strain throughout Christian thought and experience that is faithful to "the view from below," and that its rediscovery can be a potent resource for transposing theology into a new key today. We observed earlier that composers sometimes prepare their listeners for the direction in which they go after a diminished seventh, and that *at least in retrospect* we can discern such anticipations.

In that hope, let us note four examples of how a rewriting out of neglected materials from our Christian past could help anchor liberation concerns in our Christian heritage:

1. *The church until the time of Constantine* was not the defender of the *status quo* or the enabler of the Roman way of life. We have forgotten the degree to which it was a persecuted minority, catering to slaves, ordinary people without power, and many who were not only without power but were clearly not acceptable to those with power. Early on its members were described as "those who have turned the world upside down" (Acts 17:6). After three hundred years the Emperor Constantine was nevertheless able to co-opt this institution for the support of an authoritarian state designed to benefit the few rather than the many. We could learn today both from the time when Christians were an oppressed minority and also from the signs of corruption that crept in, as the church, once authenticated by the state, replaced the tattered cloak of the oppressed with the resplendent mantle of the oppressor, a persecuted church that rapidly became a persecuting church.

The exercise is not an escape from present pressures into a study of antiquity. For "the Constantinian era" ended centuries ago, and Christians are once again a minority (even a dwindling minority in relation to present rates of population increase). Our situation is remarkably like that of the early church, and we are called to shed the subsequently developed Constantinian role of siding with oppressors rather than oppressed. Acquaintance with those first three centuries could only aid us in that imperative task.[6]

2. Another period from which neglected themes need to be recov-

ered is the history of *the radical wing of the Reformation.* Most contemporary Reformation insights are drawn from Lutheran or Calvinist sources, and once a few exceptions are noted, the truth is that mainline Reformation churches were, and are, just that: "mainline," centrist, supporters of imperialism, capitalism, colonialism, and other structures that historically have been instruments of oppression to Third World groups abroad and minority groups at home. Lutheran interpretations of Romans 13 ("Let every person be subject to the governing authorities. . . . He who resists the authorities resists what God has appointed") have often legitimated tyranny, and even Calvin's permission to the "lesser magistrates" to revolt against unjust rulers is little more than a footnote in an otherwise passive view of the role of Christians in relation to structures of injustice.

By contrast, the left-wing reformation sectarian movements challenged authority unjustly procured and sustained, sought to provide alternative communitarian models for the economic and political organization of human life, embodied a commitment to "the view from below" in the face of systems and edicts from on high, and preached a millenarian vision of social equality in sharp contrast to the social hierarchies supported by Lutherans, Calvinists, and Anglicans in the burgeoning capitalist society of the time.

This is not to say that sixteenth-century sects provide adequate models for us today, or even that such experiments were fully adequate for their own day. But it is to say that the radical Reformers sought liberation for the "lower classes" from oppressive structures, and did so in ways that may provide more significant conscientization for us than the conventional Reformation sources to which we usually turn.[7]

3. There are affinities between liberation theology and *the social gospel movement* in the United States in the early twentieth century. John C. Bennett comments:

> Liberation theology today is in some respects in a line of succession from such representatives of the Social Gospel as Walter Rauschenbusch. The Social Gospel was a theology of liberation for the industrial workers of this country.[8]

Affinities between the two include the social or communal stress as a safeguard against individualistic Christianity, the stress on praxis, a methodology arising out of the human situation rather than being imposed upon it, a passionate commitment to the dispossessed, and a recognition of the systemic nature of evil. Many social gospel proponents took the socialist option seriously as a framework for restating the Christian faith, and Walter Rauschenbusch, the foremost exponent of the social gospel, was, as Robert T. Handy puts it, "generally known as a socialist," though "his socialism was mild, revisionist, evolutionary, and non-doctrinaire."[9]

Rauschenbusch's view of the systemic nature of evil deserves notice in the present discussion:

> Theology [he wrote in 1917] has not given adequate attention to the social idealizations of evil, which falsify the ethical stands for the individual by the authority of his group or community, deaden the voice of the Holy Spirit to the conscience of individuals and communities, and perpetuate antiquated wrongs in society. . . . The evils of one generation are caused by the wrongs of the generations that preceded, and will in turn condition the sufferings and temptations of those who come after.[10]

In an intriguing image, he drives the point home:

> The sheep-tick hides in the wool of the sheep and taps the blood where it flows warm and rich. But the tick has no power to alter the arterial system and to bring the aorta close to the skin where it can get at it. *Human ticks have been able to do this.* They have gained control of legislation, courts, police, military, royalty, church, property, religion, and have altered the constitution of nations in order to make things easy for the tick class. The laws, institutions, doctrines, literature, art, and manners which these ruling classes have secreted have been social means of infection which have bred new evils for generations.[11]

If Rauschenbusch and others were a little too sure that the earthly establishment of the Kingdom was not far off, such oversimplified prognostication will hardly tempt people today.[12]

4. Neglected themes within *recent European theology* can open us to liberation concerns. It is noteworthy that both Paul Tillich and Karl Barth were socialists in their earlier days. Tillich was active in

the movement for Religious Socialism after World War I, although he put his socialist leanings to one side in later life, partly no doubt, because of his forced migration to the United States after Hitler came to power, where he felt that he had little political contribution to make. It would be instructive to learn how and why this apparent disenchantment occurred, to be replaced by broader concerns with theology and culture as a whole, particularly psychiatry and the arts.[13]

The case of Barth is now the subject of fierce debate; it seems clear that Barth's earlier socialist commitments (he joined the socialist party in Switzerland in 1915) persisted to the end of his life, and there are those who argue that Barth's *Church Dogmatics* can only be understood by a recognition of his commitment to socialism as well as to Jesus Christ.[14]

Whatever the outcome of that debate, it is clear that the mature Barth retains an intense awareness of the social direction of the Biblical message. Two quotations will make the point:

> God always takes His stand unconditionally and passionately on this side and on this side alone: against the lofty and on behalf of the lowly; against those who already enjoy right and privilege and on behalf of those who are denied it and deprived of it.[15]

In a later writing, Barth spells out what this means for the church:

> The Church is witness of the fact that the Son of man came to seek and to save the lost. And this implies that . . . the Church must concentrate first on the lower and lowest levels of human society. The poor, the socially and economically weak and threatened, will always be the object of its primary and particular concern, and it will always insist on the State's special responsibility for these weaker members of society.
>
> That it will bestow its love upon them . . . [is] the most important thing; but it must not concentrate on this and neglect the other thing to which it is committed by its political responsibility; the effort to achieve such a fashioning of the law as will make it impossible for "equality before the law" to become a cloak under which strong and weak, independent and dependent, rich and poor, employers and employees, in fact receive different treatment at its hands: the weak being unduly restricted, the strong unduly protected. The church must stand for social justice in the political sphere. And in choosing between the various socialistic possibilities (social-

liberalism? co-operativism? syndicalism? free trade? moderate or radical Marxism?) it will always choose the movement from which it can expect the greatest measure of social justice (leaving all other considerations on one side).[16]

In the face of such comments, it is surely premature to cut all ties with the past and assume that we must begin *de novo*.[17]

REDIRECTING OUR NORTH AMERICAN SONG— A NEW KIND OF NATIONAL ANTHEM

We have seen that our individual story overlaps with our national story and that to many hearers of our national story it describes us as oppressors. On the other hand, we have always wanted to read our history as a history of hope: "the tired, the poor, the huddled masses" celebrated on the plaque of the Statue of Liberty came here to escape oppression and found freedom awaiting them.

Could we rehear our national song so that our future would conform more nearly to what we wish our past had been? Perhaps some symbols, events, and persons from our past have received inadequate attention, in relationship to which and to whom we could rehear our history and create a future based less on aiding oppressors than on siding with oppressed. It is important to do this *from our own heritage*, and not from some other heritage. Otherwise, as Rosemary Ruether has commented, our national symbols will be appropriated and corrupted by others; the DAR, for example, exploits the image of "revolution" in the past in order to ensure that there will be no "revolution" in the future. Robert Bellah points out that one reason socialism has failed to capture the North American imagination is because of an inherent Yankee suspicion about ideas, vocabularies, and leaders imported from Europe. Socialist concerns, he argues, must be articulated out of the distinctively American experience, if they are to gain a hearing here.[18]

John Coleman, a California Jesuit, asked a friend deeply committed to social change whom he would pick as the truly great figures of the American past. As might be imagined, the friend did not pick

Andrew Carnegie, John D. Rockefeller, Calvin Coolidge, or Henry
Luce. He did pick William Penn, Roger Williams, Thomas Jefferson,
William Lloyd Garrison, Abraham Lincoln, Eugene V. Debs, Susan
B. Anthony, Clarence Darrow, Jane Addams, Norman Thomas, Wal-
ter Reuther, Reinhold Niebuhr, Martin Luther King, and Chief
Justice Earl Warren. Asked which periods in the American past
would be most "usable" for building a creative future, the friend
responded:

> America's revolution and the early republic; the abolitionist movement;
> the populist movement of Senator Carl Schurz and William Jennings
> Bryan; the early labor movement at the turn of the century; the progres-
> sive movement, especially in its attacks on the corporate trusts and its
> attempt at cooperatives; the early years of the New Deal; the movement
> for civil rights in the 1960's.[19]

If one looks at American history from such perspectives it is possible to believe that resources for significant achievements of social
justice are available, even if one is less sanguine than Bellah and
Coleman about enlisting American "civil religion" on the side of
radical change.

A dramatic instance of drawing the nation's past to redirect the
nation's future is found in the program of the Black Panther Party.
The Panthers, who have been feared in many quarters because of
their espousal of radical change, conclude their manifesto with a call
to revolution:

> Whenever any form of government becomes destructive of these ends,
> *it is the right of the people to alter or to abolish it, and to institute new
> government,* laying its foundation on such principles and organizing its
> powers in such form, *as to them* shall seem most likely to effect their safety
> and happiness. . . . When a long train of abuses and usurpations, pursuing
> invariably the same object, evinces a design to reduce them under absolute
> despotism, *it is their right, it is their duty, to throw off such government,*
> and to provide new guards for their future security. (Italics added)

This plea for people to take matters into their own hands has
frightened many hearers; when told that the words were not by Huey

Newton or Bobby Seale but had been taken from another document, many hearers assumed that the latter was either *The Communist Manifesto* or *The Collected Writings of Karl Marx*. Few of them recognized that the quotation comes from the Declaration of Independence of the United States of America, dated July 4, 1776.

To what kind of analysis do such hints point us? One attempt at an answer is Joe Holland's *The American Journey*, a "working paper" that seeks to combine the perspectives of the American tradition, the Catholic tradition, and the Marxian tradition.[20] Examining the dilemma with which we began this section—the hiatus between American history as harbinger of hope and as instrument of oppression—Holland looks for reasons for the shift. His thesis is that *"the structures of American capitalism* (cultural, political, and economic) have kept the American struggles for freedom from bearing their richest fruit" (p. 7). He proposes that

> there is ground for cooperative solidarity between America's ordinary people and the ordinary people of the rest of the world, because both the American people and the people of other nations are exploited and manipulated by the *integrated* structures of world (not only American) capitalism. (P. 7)

The task is to find ways of creating solidarity between "the protest of exploited people of the Third World" and "the social anger of ordinary Americans" (p. 8). The oppressions to which "ordinary people" are subjected are identified as "class exploitation, imperialism, racism and sexism" (p. 9). In this perspective, Holland reexamines our history and finds it imbued with economic exploitation (from the early settlement when property rights were more important than human rights), racism (against blacks, Native Americans, and many others), sexism (the exploitation of women), and imperialism (particularly beginning in the nineteenth century).

Holland feels that the "American empire" that developed out of this is now on the decline. This is a bitter truth for Americans, but a truth nonetheless. In coping with it, he says, "we must nourish ourselves on the dreams and struggles of America's ordinary people," those who "are not willing to see its destiny handed over to a social class built on maximization of profit" (p. 94). If there is to be a true future, he concludes,

> if we as a nation are to be faithful to our historical call, then it will be because America's ordinary people—its workers, its poor, its women, its myriad races and cultures—begin to learn, in the fatigue of the journey, that we must stand together, in solidarity with each other and with all the human family. (P. 94)

Although the above summary is sketchy, it does suggest some directions in which a theological-social-political-economic analysis might take us. Out of it, "a new kind of national anthem" could emerge, one that could be sung not only by a minority of upper-class beneficiaries but also by those who are presently the casualties of privilege-oriented social structures.

Reorganizing Our Chorus—
A Search for New Alliances

Much of this book assumes a distinction between oppressor and oppressed—a distinction embedded in contemporary social analysis and in the Bible as well. It is descriptively true for those who feel oppressed, and its truth for them suggests its importance for those who have never before taken it seriously. Its impact is divisive and overwhelming: divisive, not because it creates divisions, but because it describes them with such devastating clarity; and overwhelming because it puts so many of us on the wrong side of the division, where we are overwhelmed either with guilt at being found there or with frustration at not being sure how to change things.

The time has now come when the issue must be faced: Is the last word divisive and overwhelming? Or could oppressor and oppressed relate to their world in such a way as to change the situation creatively rather than extend it destructively? We have forestalled premature appeals to the argument "But we are all oppressed . . ." on the grounds that this does not acknowledge the *degrees of oppression* that separate most of us from "the wretched of the earth." Let us now assume that we are not raising the issue prematurely, and see whether we can deal honestly with it.

We discover initially that most people do stand on both sides of the hyphen dividing oppressor-oppressed. Blacks in Harlem feel oppressed by whites; but Puerto Rican immigrants to Harlem often feel oppressed by blacks. Latin-American men feel oppressed by economic structures; but Latin-American women feel oppressed by men who use *machismo* to oppress women. North American university students feel oppressed by demands of upward mobility, fearing that they will be victimized by a system that encourages them, so many believe, to hedge, fudge, dissimulate, connive, lie, cheat, and steal in order to make it to the top. As one of them put it, "So you win the rat race, you're still a rat." All of this is real, even though the victimized are more likely to seek a psychiatrist than organize a revolution.

Thomas Ambrogi, out of conferences on this problem in California, has drawn some interesting conclusions:[21]

The basis for conscientization of all people is an acknowledgment that they are being hurt. "If we live our lives oppressing and exploiting others, then that must dehumanize us and it must be hurting us. If we live our lives being oppressed and exploited, then that must be hurting and dehumanizing us." In both cases, people are being hurt and dehumanized. When we discover the pain that is hurting *us*, we can be effectively mobilized for action. "Determined action cannot be sustained with militancy, passion, and surety of purpose without an awareness of one's own stake in the issue." Such insight recognizes the reality of the bias toward self that we call human sin, and avoids the particular sin of intellectualizing about the pain of others. If there is pain for all of us, it is important to discover who is inflicting the pain: who is the enemy?

Is it possible that we have a common enemy, that our own sense of being oppressed and exploited has the same source as the oppression and exploitation that is experienced by peoples of the Third World? If this is so, then there is a basis for solidarity in struggle since the struggle is a common one. If this is not so, then there is no basis for solidarity in struggle; any presumed solidarity is contrived and intellectualized.

The logic of the above paragraphs must not be transformed into a new version of the argument that "the enemy of my enemy is my friend." U.S. foreign policy has often followed this logic to disastrous ends by wooing "enemies of communism" and being forced into embrace with military fascists. But when there are common concerns, such as containing human pain and overcoming human oppression, it helps to discover who or what is inhibiting the achievement of such concerns.

Here are some illustrations of the possibility of breaking through the oppressor-oppressed dialectic. Basil Moore, writing out of the South African struggle, comments:

> I am prepared to trust and stand alongside a man who is fighting *for himself and his own freedom,* if I know that his freedom is bound up with mine. I cannot wholeheartedly trust a man who is fighting *for me,* for I fear that sooner or later he will tire of the struggle.[22]

A black friend, commenting about white people who want to "work for blacks," recently said to me: "You people must realize that you've got some oppression on you too, and I'll trust you a lot more if you have a stake in getting somebody off *your* back than if you are simply trying to get someone off *my* back. Because in the latter case you may find more interesting things to do and leave me in the lurch." Elaine Brown, a leader of the Black Panther Party, put it this way in talking to members of a white suburban church nearby: "You folks act as if everything that happens to us were your fault. Well, some of it is, but you'd better realize that anybody in this room who isn't making over $25,000 a year doesn't have any more power than we do. You may *think* you do, but you don't. Just try changing the basic structures of the Bay Area economy! *All* of us are being ripped off by power structures we don't control. And unless all of us join forces, black and white, poor and not-so-poor, we'll never make a dent on those who are controlling our lives."

If oppressors also suffer various forms of oppression, then we must ask how they are going to be freed. Those who suffer the greatest oppressions in our society are responding that *the oppressors cannot free themselves, but can only be freed by the oppressed.* James Cone, an American black theologian, writes:

> When the oppressed affirm their freedom by refusing to behave according to the masters' rules, they not only liberate themselves from oppression,

but they also liberate the oppressors from an enslavement to their illusions.[23]

No one has developed this insight more powerfully than Paulo Freire, a Brazilian educator who has been expelled from three countries for the revolutionary act of helping people to learn to read. (Military dictators recognize that literacy is a revolutionary challenge to tyranny.) Freire comments:

> As the oppressors dehumanize others and violate their rights, they themselves also become dehumanized. As the oppressed, fighting to be human, take away the oppressors' power to dominate and suppress, they restore to the oppressors the humanity they had lost in the exercise of oppression.
> It is only the oppressed who, by freeing themselves, free their oppressors. The latter, as an oppressive class, can free neither others nor themselves.[24]

Gutiérrez, relating the discussion explicitly to the Christian command to love, writes:

> One loves the oppressors by liberating them from their inhuman condition as oppressors, by liberating them from themselves. But this cannot be achieved except by resolutely opting for the oppressed, that is, by combatting the oppressive classes.[25]

He later cites a widely quoted statement by Guilio Girardi:

> We must love everyone, but it is not possible to love everyone in the same way; we love the oppressed by liberating them; we love the oppressors by fighting them. We love the oppressed by liberating them from their misery, and the oppressors by liberating them from their sin.[26]

We are not dealing with sentimentalized love, but with love-in-conflict, love that takes sides, love that seeks to pull down evil structures so that it can build up people no longer dominated and dehumanized by those structures, no matter on which side of the oppressor-oppressed dialectic they began. This theme—that the oppressed in acting to liberate themselves also liberate their oppressors—is consistent with the Christian notion that strength is made perfect through weakness, and that it takes the weak to deliver the strong—a truth not only enacted on the cross but recapitulated analogously whenever the "despised and rejected" are instruments of liberation for the high and mighty.

But there is a role for oppressors as well; they are not simply to wait passively for deliverance. Again it is Freire who encapsulates an important truth:

> The oppressor is solidary with the oppressed only when he stops regarding the oppressed as an abstract category and sees them as persons who have been unjustly dealt with, deprived of their voice, cheated in the sale of their labor—when he stops making pious, sentimental, and individualistic gestures and risks an act of love. True solidarity is found only in the plenitude of this act of love, in its existentiality, in its praxis.[27]

The "act of love," the attempt at solidarity, must not be romantically or individualistically conceived. White people can never know what it means to be black, nor can North American middle-class people become those who live on Native American "reservations." But they could get a new idea of what it means to be white, so that, freed from immobilizing guilt, they could, out of this new understanding, act responsibly in solidarity with blacks or Native Americans. Benjamin Reist has given some important clues in *Theology in Red, White, and Black.* The task for whites, he asserts, is not to play at being blacks or Native Americans, but to be whites with a new sense of what it means to be white. In the past to be white meant to dominate, to be in charge, to run the show. In the present, however, whites can be liberated from the oppressor role by pressure from blacks and reds (and globally from browns and yellows as well), discovering that being white *now* means being part of a human mosaic—not chief part any longer, but just one part—and no longer needing to feel guilty or ashamed of being white, because in the new understanding one can be brother or sister rather than oppressor. As Reist puts it:

> The road to inexhaustible freedom for whites involves becoming neither black nor red, but *white,* for the first time. It involves becoming white as liberated into particularity, the particularity of being *one* component in the full mosaic that is humanity; becoming white in such a way that white cannot be white unless red and black are equally present in the historical

space that is human liberation; becoming white in such a way that even along with red and black the triangle is a fragment, hoping and working for transmutation into the pentagram that is red, white, black, brown, and yellow. . . . We must contend that the liberation of the gospel for whites involves becoming white in ways no living memory enshrines, for it involves whiteness as one *ethnic* component among the sweep of five.[28]

This means that unless all are free, none are free. The oppressed who win their freedom from the oppressors only to end up becoming oppressors themselves have not achieved liberation; they have merely exchanged one kind of bondage for another, though it is certainly understandable that they prefer the latter to the former. The oppressors who fight to the end against giving up their power remain enslaved too; in destroying others they destroy themselves. As Freire insists, the freedom of the oppressed involves the freedom of the oppressor as well; as Martin Luther King insisted, the day when blacks are finally free will be the day when whites are finally free; as leaders of women's liberation insist, freeing women is also a way of freeing men.

Are there any "common struggles" in which all could engage together that would attack the systemic evil that in various degrees holds everyone enslaved? Let us note three typical concerns where people starting from different places could work toward mutually liberating ends:

1. *Shared concerns about work.* Many in the oppressor class hate their work. They consider it destructive of meaning for their lives, of their human psyches, of family relations, of values that have to be subordinated to "business is business," of the environment around them. All this, even though they are getting paid very well. So they hate the work they are doing, and, perhaps without really being aware of it, they hate the system that forces them to live that way. They would like to find new work patterns.

Many in the oppressed class hate their work too, or, more likely, hate the fact that the system denies them the possibility to work at all. They too consider their work, or lack of it, destructive of meaning for their lives, not only of human psyches but of human bodies as well, of family relations since their families are starving, of values that have to be subordinated to "anything for a piece of bread," of both the physical and the human environment around them. All this, on top of which they are getting paid very little, or nothing at all. So they too hate the work they are doing, or hate the fact that there is no work they can do, and, often being very much aware of it, they hate the system that forces them to live that way. They too would like to find new work patterns—patterns that not only provide jobs but provide jobs that pay enough to live on and give a sense of meaning and dignity to life.

The parallels are not merely contrived. Work is an issue in relation to which so-called oppressors and oppressed share some common concerns. It is at least conceivable that some "new alliances" could be created—if enough people determined that work patterns should be set by the workers themselves rather than by somebody else, and that patterns based on workers' rights rather than corporation profits were both possible and crucial. Conscienticizing along these lines could begin a significant revolution challenging a system that makes workers, all up and down the line, cower before the decisions of a handful who presently decide what is to happen to all the rest.

2. *Shared concerns about power.* Changing work patterns is partly a matter of challenging existing power structures. The challenging of power structures must move to other areas as well. The maldistribution of power is a problem for Latin Americans, blacks, Asians, Africans, and women. It is also a problem for North Americans, whites, Europeans, and men. But the problem is seen in different ways by the two groups: the problem for the first is that *they don't have enough power,* while the problem for the second is that *they have too much.*

Too little power makes it almost impossible to act creatively, or even get things done—as Third World peoples know full well. Too much power makes it almost inevitable that power will be used for one's own ends and at the expense of needs of others—as Third World peoples also know full well, since they are victims.

Can power be used creatively, or is it inevitably going to be used destructively? Clearly, it can be used creatively only if there are some *limitations* on who uses how much for what ends. But those with power resist relinquishing it voluntarily. Efforts to make them share it lead them to hoard it even more.

The dilemma cannot be solved by letting those with inordinate power retain it, trusting them to use it wisely—a solution those with power widely espouse. The rest will not trust them, and rightly so, since it will *not* be used wisely. Nor is power in our day automatically going to shift to those who had none before. Even if this happened, the same problems would remain; they would simply be acted out with a different cast of characters. There must be some kind of mutuality of shared power. This involves danger, since those without power will have to combine forces in order to be taken seriously by those with power, and such a combination of forces is very accident-prone. Those in powerful nations who feel the urgency of the problem will have to work against the presumed self-interest of their own countries—a role that does not enhance popularity. This will be a testing point of the possibility of forming alliances of creative solidarity across the oppressor-oppressed dialectic.[29]

3. *Common concern about human rights.* Almost all persons share a concern about violations of *individual* human rights—the right to speak, to write, to protest, to be free from unjust imprisonment, torture, and so on. These rights have been grossly violated in many parts of Latin America, where political dissidents are arrested, tortured, killed, or simply "disappear." People elsewhere have made significant attempts, through such groups as Amnesty International and the use of political pressure, to eliminate the violation of individual human rights. To many, particularly in affluent countries, this seems the sum and substance of the human rights issue.

In reality, it is only the beginning of the human rights issue. Third World countries have had to remind affluent countries that what is at stake is not simply individual human rights, but *social* human rights as well. If it could be established tomorrow that there was no longer a single political prisoner in Latin America, that would be a cause for rejoicing, but it would not signal the end of the human rights struggle. For social human rights are crucial too—the right food, shelter, education, medical care, decent housing. Affluent societies often do not look on these as "rights"; those in power can purchase them and thus take them for granted, failing to realize that they are beyond the reach of most of the human family.

So this is another arena for "new alliances," recognizing that here too none are free until all are free, and recognizing that the structures of our society thrive on just these inequities: if tyrannies suppress individual human rights, "democracies" resist the establishment of social human rights (calling them "socialistic" or "communistic"). All societies must work for a balance between individual and social human rights, for either at the expense of the other is less than tolerable. We need to have the logs in our own eyes exposed, as well as calling attention to the specks in the eyes of others.[30]

Our search for new alliances makes clear that the search is a communal one, and that we must break through barriers that have previously separated us—oppressor-oppressed, black-white, north-south, bourgeois-proletariat, or whatever.

But there is one communal front we have not yet explored—the Christian church. Are new alliances possible here, not only kinship with beleaguered friends in Uruguay or Chile, but comrades-in-arms in First Presbyterian Church in Wichita or Second Baptist Church in Houston or All Saints Episcopal Church in Croton Heights? To search for such alliances is obvious: Christians are called to be Christians in community, not in solitude. But the search is also precarious: churches are not frequently on the forefront of change. Often they are bastions of the *status quo,* which means that they are complicit in structures of injustice. Prophets, moreover, are least honored among their own, as Amos discovered at Bethel and Jesus discovered at Nazareth. In what ways, if at all, can we expect churches to hear the theology in a new key and join in the new song? That is the question to which we must turn in conclusion.

CHAPTER 6

Two Cheers for the Church: A Not-Quite Hallelujah Chorus

(Is There Still a Role for the Church?)

> It would be naive to imagine that liberation theology can be accepted in any consistent or serious way by the ecclesiastical structures now in existence.
> —Juan Luis Segundo, *The Liberation of Theology*, p. 139

E. M. Forster and George Friedrich Handel would seem to have little in common: Forster was not involved in the church, Handel wrote involved church music. And yet the former can help us appropriate the latter more creatively. Forster wrote a book called *Two Cheers for Democracy*, the title of which suggests restrained enthusiasm. And Handel, partway through *The Messiah*, wrote a "Hallelujah Chorus" that epitomizes unrestrained enthusiasm. Forster's mood will serve our purposes better than Handel's. For while it would be pleasant to conclude with a triumphant assertion that "the church is the answer," we cannot do so since, to whatever degree that is true, it is also true (as Segundo suggests) that the church is part of the problem. So any "Hallelujah Chorus" must be muted. There can be some rejoicing, but not too much.

This is not all loss. An unrestrained series of "Hallelujahs" is not particularly edifying. Even Handel's chorus tends to pall, its opening measures consisting of nothing but the word "Hallelujah" double fortissimo ten times in a row. Why the king stood during its initial performance is shrouded in mystery. Perhaps he merely wanted to stretch; how could he have known ahead of time that the chorus would be worthy of honor? At all events, if we stand metaphorically in response to what we have heard from liberation theologians, it is not so much to pay tribute to them as to declare, "There's a job to be done. We'd like to enlist in the struggle"—a declaration better made on one's feet than in an armchair.

There *is* a chorus to be sung, but it is the anticipation of this chapter that it will not be sung by all. It will, we must hope, be sung by a creative minority that will continue to invite others, even though many will continue to decline the invitation.

Scenarios for the Future

Is such a conclusion too pessimistic? Let us examine some ways to relate to the church in the light of liberation concerns.[1] Taking seriously Segundo's conviction that present ecclesiastical structures will resist liberation theology, we face a variety of possibilities:

One scenario would propose that for the sake of a new social order in the light of the gospel we must *leave the church*, since in Martin Luther King's image, the church has become a thermometer rather than a thermostat, recording the climate around it, rather than changing it.

Those who choose to leave usually seek alternative communities in which commitment to liberation for the oppressed seems more possible than it is within unwieldy ecclesiastical structures. They affirm a *sectarian* model—a voluntary community made up of the truly committed, choosing to withdraw from the rest.

Two things must be said about those who make this choice: *(a)* They may be right. They may see things more clearly than the rest of us and possess a higher quotient of courage in acting on what they see. At the very least, they can keep us off-balance if we remain within the ponderous edifice that is their despair. *(b)* We must honor the complaint many of them would voice that they are being falsely described as having "left the church." The true community of believers, trying to live in costly obedience to Jesus Christ, can exist where only two or three are gathered together; it does not need bishops or buildings or boards or budgets. "The church" in our day may be found outside official structures far more than it is found within.

Everyone who opts to remain within the church must have faced seriously the option of leaving. Otherwise he or she will have ignored, or at least trivialized, the degree to which institutional Christianity has been a willing partner in maintaining structures of injustice.

A second scenario opts to *accept the church as it is*, "warts and all," affirming that if it cannot make things a lot better, it can at least keep them from getting a lot worse. Advocates of this position settle for modest victories and argue realistically that since the church is made up of sinners it can hardly be expected to act like a society of saints.

It is easy to stand in judgment upon such a position until we realize that it describes most of us. We make our peace with the institution, live within it, and feel vindicated when we can point to a small reformist victory. But if we have truly heard the cries of pain to which this book is trying to listen, we will be increasingly uneasy at the degree of capitulation the scenario proposes.

A third scenario would declare forthrightly that the church's task is misconceived when the changing of society becomes its concern. Proponents of this scenario insist that the true task of the church is *to turn inward*, a position we have alluded to before and need not elaborate again. Such privatization of religion appears the most likely scenario for North American organized religion in the coming years. It will dwell on "the mistakes of the '60s," emphasize "spiritual values," and offer protection against an increasingly clamorous and bitter world outside. If thicker church walls are needed to keep out the cries of anguish, thicker they will become; there are always resources for such rebuilding.

By a curious redefinition, adherents of this growing group will claim to be the true "church," when in fact they are becoming more "sectarian" than adherents of our first scenario, since they are cutting themselves off from a great body of Christians *elsewhere in the world* who cannot afford the luxury of a privatized faith, and also are denying the sweep of Biblical and Christian social concern of which liberation theology has been reminding us. They may become the true "separatists" of our day, giving comfort to those in power, but becoming separated from the majority of the human family who need material as well as spiritual food.

A final scenario would propose *becoming a self-conscious minority within the church, realizing that the church must become a self-conscious minority within the world.* This means taking the Biblical image of "the remnant," the handful within the church committed to God's liberating purposes, and straining it almost to the breaking point by attempting to be "the remnant within the remnant," the handful within the handful—those who opt neither to get out nor to stay complacently within, but to search for ways to keep a critical allegiance to what the church ought to be in spite of what it is.

This scenario could become a normative image for the future of the church.

IMAGES FOR THE FUTURE

We live by images. Whether television advertising is confronting us with The Cheerful Housewife, spiritually fulfilled by her eagerly shared discovery that Brand X cleans her sink better than Brand Y, or The Omnicompetent Male, leaving his executive suite for a skiing weekend thanks to possessing the appropriate credit card, we are offered images on which to model ourselves. In more profound ways, Grünewald paints a repugnant image of a dying Christ in whose grisly execution we are to believe that the redemption of the world has taken place, while Robert Frost describes swaying birch trees in ways reminiscent of a woman bending over as she combs her hair.

The importance of images is that they are *suggestive rather than exhaustive.* They trigger responses that go beyond what they visually or verbally convey. After they have served that purpose they can be discarded or replaced by more adequate ones.

This is the function of the three images we shall examine. Proceeding from a variety of viewpoints, they are meant to suggest a common focus. They are suggestive rather than exhaustive.

1. The Remnant Within the Remnant

By taking "the remnant within the remnant" as our normative image, we align ourselves with Segundo in believing that liberation theology will not be accepted "by the ecclesiastical structures now in existence," but we seek to salvage from that conclusion a possibility that others who are not primarily beholden to ecclesiastical structures may be more open. Acknowledging that rather than being a majority of the human family we are now a minority, a "remnant," we affirm the need for a remnant within *that* remnant to embody the liberation message of the Scriptures.

This is not a counsel of despair; it is consistent with the prophetic role since the earliest records available to us. In 700 B.C. when Amos inveighed against civil, ecclesiastical, and structural corruption, pointing out that the Day of the Lord would be darkness and not light, he set forth an alternative, exhorting his hearers to "hate evil, and love good, and establish justice in the gate." And yet, the most he promised was that if these injunctions were followed, "it *may* be that the Lord, the God of hosts, will be gracious to *the remnant* of Joseph" (Amos 5:15, italics added). A conditional possibility for a few. Two cheers for the church.

Those who embrace the remnant image today will lead apparently split lives. They will have one foot in the institution, with all its complacency in the face of evil and all its complicity in the ongoing-ness of evil, but they will have the other foot somewhere else—in various *ad hoc* groups that transcend denominational, ecclesiastical, racial, class, and even faith lines, groups dedicated to this or that aspect of the liberation struggle. There was a foreshadowing of this in the early '60s around the civil rights struggle, and in the later '60s and early '70s around protest against continuing American slaughter in Southeast Asia. There will need to be new rallying points for the late '70s and early '80s and we shall look at some of them shortly.

What keeps the split loyalty from becoming destructively schizophrenic is the fact that individuals so positioned can be intermediaries between both groups. Allegiance to the church can provide wisdom for the *ad hoc* affiliations, and allegiance to the *ad hoc* affiliations can provide leaven within cautious ecclesiastical structures. To affirm both allegiances will be one contrition of "the remnant within the remnant."[2]

There is a serious danger in this image: it is the danger of elitism, of becoming precious, private, and proud, assuming that there is a special role that only special people can play, and that they had better be chosen with special care. In such a position there is always a temptation to ignore "the masses" for the sake of "the few." The dilemma can be overcome only by remembering that "the remnant within the remnant" is not created for the self-indulgence of a tiny constituency but for the sake of greater authenticity of the whole. The Biblical images of "little flock" and "the multitudes" exist *for each other,* as Joseph Ratzinger has pointed out. The division within the Bible avoids elitism, since the remnant has an obligation beyond itself to others:

> God does not divide humanity thus (the "many" and the "few") to save the few and hurl the many into perdition. Nor does he do it to save the many *in an easy way* and the few *in a hard way.* Instead we could say that he uses the numerical few as a leverage point for raising up the many.[3]

2. The Abrahamic Minority

The image of the church as "the Abrahamic minority" is associated particularly with Dom Helder Câmara, archbishop of Recife, Brazil, although its origins, of course, are Biblical, deriving mainly from Genesis and Hebrews 11 and 12. Dom Helder's use of this image deepens our understanding of "the remnant within the remnant."[4]

Abraham was the one who had to venture forth "not knowing wither he went," acting against the obviously sound advice to stay where he was, since he already had flocks, wives, grazing land, and all the rest. Nevertheless he obeyed the call to go to new and unexplored places. It is this venturesomeness for which Dom Helder calls today. He speaks optimistically of a group to be called Action for Justice and Peace:

> Everywhere there are minorities capable of understanding Action for Justice and Peace and adopting it as a workshop for study and action. Let us call these minorities the Abrahamic minorities, because like Abraham, we are hoping against all hope.
>
> Do you think you are alone? Look around you. Talk to your friends. Talk

to people in your house, in your neighborhood, at your school, at your work, with your leisure companions. You will be surprised to discover that your "Abrahamic minority" already exists. And you were unaware of it.[5]

It had been Dom Helder's hope that the movement would take hold within the church itself, but a few years after writing the above lines he confessed that while the original hope was ill-founded he had subsequently found a much wider community for whom the term "Abrahamic minority" was appropriate:

I now realize that it is virtually useless to appeal to institutions as such [but] everywhere I go . . . I find minorities with the power for love and justice which could be likened to nuclear energy locked for millions of years in the smallest atoms and waiting to be released.[6]

Everywhere he went, he reports, he discovered minorities, "men and women born to serve their neighbor, ready for any sacrifice if it helps to build at last a really juster and more human world" (p. 4). Although these people live in their own environments, they think of themselves as part of the total human family.

It is the Abrahamic minority who will hear the cries of the oppressed and recognize those cries as "the voice of God." It is the Abrahamic minority who will be committed to "the most important task in our century, to free those two out of three (persons) who are still in slavery, even though they are no longer called slaves" (p. 21). It is the Abrahamic minority who will recognize that "poverty makes people subhuman. Excess of wealth makes people inhuman" (p. 32). So the clarion call is: "Abrahamic Minorities Unite!" Those who feel that they belong to this family "do not wait for permission to act" (p. 43). All kinds of allegiances are possible, within the churches, between the churches, outside the churches. The membership can be very wide; its membership test is simply that one who feels that he or she belongs within it "should not remain alone" (p. 43).

3. The Freedom of the Anti-Chameleon

To clarify further the posture of "the remnant within the remnant" let us appropriate a sequence developed by Jürgen Moltmann:[7]

Surveying the history of theology in the church, Moltmann observes a long period of *fossil theology*, i.e., the retention of an imprint from the past, usually the distant past, which was safe from transformation, since any attempt to change a fossil destroys it. In reaction to this, theology in the recent past became *chameleon theology*, imitating the animal who, rather than being unchanging like a fossil, changes all the time, adapting its color to match its environment, with the aim of being as indistinguishable as possible. In contradistinction to such culture-affirming religion, Moltmann argues for an *anti-chameleon theology*, i.e., a theology that is as sharply distinguished as possible from its background and surroundings, standing in vivid contrast to the patterns of its age. This is surely how Dom Helder defines the role of "the Abrahamic minority," and it is what the Roman Catholic bishops at Medellín were seeking when they wrote:

> In our evaluation of popular religion, we must not take as our frame of reference the westernized culture interpretations of the middle and upper classes; rather we must judge its meaning in the context of the sub-cultures of the rural and marginal urban groups.[8]

"The remnant within the remnant" must be distinguished from rather than blended into its surroundings, whether those surroundings are culture or church or both. This can begin to provide the liberation, or "freedom of the anti-chameleon," to express solidarity with the oppressed.

Beyond Sloganeering: Can We Enter Into "Solidarity with the Oppressed"?

We now come to the most difficult task of all. For we must use words to describe the necessity of deeds, and it is notoriously easy to let words go bail for deeds. The task of "the remnant within the remnant" is clear: it is to enter into "solidarity with the oppressed," but the ease with which the phrase is commandeered suggests that we are likely to settle for sloganeering rather than commitment.

Nevertheless, the effort must be made, and we shall now propose five ingredients that might begin to lessen the distance between where we are and where we know we should be.

1. Denunciation and Annunciation

The first ingredient proposes the overall vocation of "the remnant within the remnant" as denunciation and annunciation. Paulo Freire speaks of the need for

> denunciation of a dehumanizing reality and annunciation of its transcendence by another reality in which [persons] will be more fully human. ... The acts of denunciation and annunciation must be, not empty words, but historical commitments. Denunciation and annunciation are possible only through praxis, just as it is only through praxis that one can realize the "announcement" proclaimed in the denunciation.[9]

Within this compressed statement are a number of themes that we must elaborate briefly:

First, neutrality is not a possibility. The decision to stand above the battle, or to one side, or to minister equally to all participants, is already a taking of sides. Such presumed neutrality will only reinforce the *status quo*. To denounce is not to take sides for the first time; it is simply to indicate which side one is already on.

Second, the denunciation is not merely word but deed as well, targeted against "every dehumanizing situation, which is contrary to brotherhood, justice and liberty."[10] While this will involve speaking, it will also involve acting on the basis of speaking. If Christians denounce an unjust regime, that may mean refusing to pay taxes to support it; if a church denounces torture, that may mean public exposure of the torturers and banning them from the Eucharist; if a church denounces an exploitive economy, that may mean refusing to profit from the economy and becoming "the poor church."

Third, the church must not only denounce dehumanizing situations created by others; it must also "criticize every sacralization of oppressive structures to which the Church itself might have contributed."[11] The church has been very good at sacralizing oppressive structures and failing to acknowledge its own complicity in the evil those structures perpetuate. Failure to "denounce" in the early years of the Vietnam war made the churches complicit in the "war crimes" committed there by the United States; lack of denunciation of church investment policies makes Christian institutions complicit in apartheid in South Africa, economic oppression in the Dominican Republic and West Virginia, and the regressive activities of the Chilean junta. Occasional denunciations by "remnants within the remnant" are minute in comparison to the magnitude of the problems.

Fourth, denunciation must attack the *causes* of injustice and not just the *consequences.* If wages are below poverty level in a Third World country or an area of the United States, it is not enough to deplore the fact; the analysis must indicate why this is so, even if (or especially if) it turns out that U.S. business interests pay exploitive wages in order to keep stockholders happy at the annual meeting.

Fifth, since negation implies affirmation, those who denounce must indicate the annunciatory stance from which they speak. Denunciation of exploitation by the rich is an annunciation of the gospel's special concern for the poor; denunciation of a competitive economy is an annunciation that a cooperative economy would be closer to the demands of the gospel. So annunciations are also the task of the church. Sometimes they proceed from utopian visions—we "announce" the way we think life should be and denounce what falls short or impedes the vision. For the church, annunciations proceed from proclamations of the nature of the Kingdom of God. The fact that the Biblical vision of the Kingdom stresses the exaltation of the poor, for example, furnishes material for reflection and action on the part of "the remnant within the remnant." Such annunciation will not only offer alternatives to present evil structures, but will stand as an ongoing check against complacency, however evil or good the structures become. As Gutiérrez puts it:

> The Gospel annunciation opens human history to the future promised by God and reveals his present work. On the one hand, this annunciation will indicate that in every achievement of brotherhood and justice among men there is a step toward total communion. By the same token, it will indicate

the incomplete and provisional character of any and every human achievement.[12]

Sixth, annunciation, like denunciation, must be lived rather than merely spoken. This has politicized consequences:

> The annunciation of the Gospel, precisely insofar as it is a message of total love, has an inescapable political dimension, because it is addressed to people who live within a fabric of social relationships, which, in our case, keep them in a subhuman condition.[13]

Seventh, the time between denunciation and annunciation is (as Freire has remarked) *the time for building,* the time for the doing of deeds that will illustrate the annunciatory stance and the consequent denunciation that must come from it. The time for building will be the time *(a)* for acts of solidarity with the oppressed wherever they are, inside or outside the church, *(b)* for helping the voiceless gain a voice of their own, *(c)* for taking sides politically, and finally, *(d)* for the development among the affluent of a theology of relinquishment, or "letting go." We now turn to a brief discussion of each of these.

2. Acts of Solidarity Within the Community

Since reformers and revolutionaries are often more interested in challenging evils far away than those near at hand, let us begin with the church itself. Everyone has a collection of ecclesiastical diseases to which the denunciation-annunciation scalpel should be applied. Where should "the remnant within the remnant" exert leverage on the rest of the Christian community? Who, in fact, are the oppressed within the church?

By any standard of accountability *women* are close to the top of the list. They have been at the center of the church's life from the beginning, and even Paul, whose male chauvinist image is uncontested, acknowledges their importance to early church life in letter after letter. But their influence has almost always been "unofficial." Until recently, women played virtually no role within the structural life of the community—deaconesses here and there, but not ministers, priests, bishops, denominational executives, or theologians. Such tasks were reserved for men.

Although this is beginning to change, it is only because women themselves have begun to exert pressure. Male resistance to new roles is appalling. Some of the arguments urged against the ordination of women are almost beyond belief in their unquestioned assurance that a certain type of genital construction is the *sine qua non* of priesthood.

Although seminaries have generally opened their doors to women, this is only the beginning of the church's obligation; it will be hollow gain to educate women for church responsibilities if the churches refuse to hire them. We will know how serious the churches are when women begin to be hired not just as assistants or associates but as senior pastors with men working under them.

It is paternalistic for a man to speak on behalf of the need for liberation of women in the churches; the voices and the leadership that will make the difference are voices and leadership emerging out of the women's ranks themselves, and they are the ones to whom the rest of us must listen.[14]

A second oppressed group within the churches are members of *ethnic minorities,* and most of what is true about discrimination against women applies *mutatis mutandis* to ethnic minorities as well. Members of these groups have also developed spokespersons, and do not need whites to represent them. Blacks in particular are blessed with articulate leaders who, by the vigor of their language and the strength of their pressure, are forcing white male leadership to take them seriously. The black theology that is developing out of this group may well be the most distinctive contribution that the United States has made to the theological enterprise.[15]

But there are other ethnic minorities as well: Chicanos, Japanese Americans, Native Americans, Puerto Ricans, Middle Europeans, and so forth. Some of these groups have decided that their own ethnic integrity demands ethnic churches which, however, are still often dependent for financial survival on the largess of the entire denomination. Blacks in particular made certain specific demands on the white ecclesiastical establishment in the '60s, particularly in a document called the "Black Manifesto," asking for reparations and other compensatory acts that were so scary to establishment whites that the demands of the document still remain an unfinished piece of business. Part of the present difficulty in confronting the oppression of ethnic minorities is that the churches, who did engage in considerable commitment and identification during the civil rights era, have now pulled back from this area. This has led some naive whites to assume that the agenda has been completed, when it is apparent to all but the most naive members of minority groups that the agenda has scarcely been initiated.

Both women and ethnic minority groups have, as already noted, been raising up their own leaders and pressing their own demands for liberation. But there are others who, although often part of such groups, deserve fuller attention, since they do not yet have a nationally focused leadership. Homosexuals, political radicals, the physically and mentally handicapped have often received such intemperate treatment from the churches that Christ's open-ended invitation appears to have been amended by his followers: "Come unto me, all ye that labor and are heavy laden, and I will give you rest (except, of course, for gays, people with leftist leanings, women who want too much to be ordained, and all social misfits who clearly belong somewhere else)."

Among those still being oppressed in church and nation, we will focus on *the economically deprived,* or less euphemistically, the poor. With all its wealth, the United States has always had pockets of poverty, areas that remain poor in part because their resources and people are exploited by the rich. One of these areas, Appalachia, has been the focus of recent attention by a Roman Catholic "remnant within the remnant," and the result of work by sisters, priests, and small groups of dedicated laypersons was the creation of a document signed by twenty-five bishops in the area, entitled "This Land Is Home to Me: A Pastoral Letter on Powerlessness in Appalachia."[16] The document is an attempt by a small group within the church to make common cause with the poor, by listening to their cries, identifying the *real* sources of oppression, reflecting on these discoveries in the light of the Biblical message, and making specific suggestions for redressing the wrong. It deserves attention here as a specific example of doing liberation theology in North America.

Psalm 72 provides a Biblical context for proclaiming the gospel in poverty-stricken Appalachia:

> The King's Son . . .
> Shall govern your people with justice
>   and your afflicted ones with judgment.
> The mountains shall yield peace for the people,
>   and the hills justice.
> HE SHALL DEFEND THE AFFLICTED . . .
> SAVE THE CHILDREN OF THE POOR,
> AND CRUSH THE OPPRESSOR.
>   Psalm 72:2–4

The bishops begin by listening

> to the cries of powerlessness
> from the region called Appalachia.
> We have listened to these cries
> and now we lend our own voice.

Part I describes "the land and its people," recognizing that whatever the variety of products and possibilities, "coal is central." Coal is not king, however:

> The kings are those who control big coal
> and the profit and power
> which comes with it.
> Many of these kings
> don't live in the region.

During the years of intensive coal mining, the workers were exploited by the coal companies and the unions. When the mines began to close and the people went to the cities, jobs were few.

When the "energy crisis" came, the corporations began to look back toward Appalachia. But it was already clear that while the corporations would profit, the people would not. They would face only "the powerlessness of isolated little people/in the face of the most powerful corporate giants/on this earth." A section on "the worship of an idol" describes "technological rationalization" (extravagant promises about the blessing technology will bring) and "max-imization of profit" (which "overwhelms the good intentions of noble people"):

> It forces them to compete brutally
> with one another.
> It pushes people into
> "conspicuous consumption"
> and "planned obsolescence."
> It delivers up control
> to a tiny minority
> whose values then shape
> our social structure.

The bishops can only conclude

> that the present economic order
> does not care for its people.
> In fact,
> profit and people frequently are contradictory.

Various reform movements are already at work, but to be effective they must combine to achieve "citizen involvement."

> The main task for such citizen involvement
> will be to build social structures
> which will provide full employment
> and decent wages
> for all people.

This will be necessary to combat the massive economic forces that are "still accountable to no one," so that while "plain people ... can't make ends meet,"

> corporate profits
> for the giant conglomerates,
> who control our energy resources,
> keep on skyrocketing.

The denunciation turns to annunciation in Part II, "The Answer of the Lord and His Church," and it provides an excellent summary of liberation themes. Stress is placed on the Biblical affirmation that

God is "the God of the poor," who not only liberates but defends "all those who are victims of injustice." The God of Israel's past is affirmed as the God of Appalachia's present, who "frees the oppressed." God's gift to us, Jesus the Messiah, is "the messiah of the poor," as Jesus' sermon in Nazareth made clear.

A section on "The Church's Social Teaching" traces the journey from *Rerum Novarum* to the present, building to an unequivocal conclusion:

> Thus,
> There must be no doubt,
> that we . . .
> can only become
> advocates of the poor.

How is this to be done? Part III initiates a conversation to which the people must respond. There must be "closeness to the people," which means continual listening, "especially to the poor," but also to the "plain people" neither rich nor poor, and finally "a challenge to the rich," the goal of which will be

> . . . citizen control
> or community control.
> The people themselves
> must shape their own destiny.

In the necessary use of scientific tools of analysis, there must be a recognition that "scientific models are not value free," and can be used "to oppress rather than liberate." Such tools must be self-consciously employed "in the service of justice."

There must be "a steeping in the presence of the Spirit." This is not merely episcopal rhetoric. For

> we know that if this renewed presence
> can mature into a convergence
> with a thirst for justice,
> a new Pentecost will truly be upon us.

There must be "Centers for Reflection and Prayer," which will do two things: first,

integrate the analytical social science skills
and the profound spirituality
necessary for persevering creatively
in the struggle for justice

and second,

link fragmented struggles
. . . with the richness of a wider national
and international network.

The bishops seek to cooperate with members of other institutions in the region (university people, economists, artists, and so forth) in attacking these problems,

provided they are open
to the voice of the poor.

They urge the creation of "Centers of Popular Culture" in every parish;

places where the poor feel welcome . . .
so that if a new society is to be born
it will emerge from the grass roots.

In such centers, emphasis must be placed on economic questions; people must learn, for example, about the power of "multinational corporations now within our region," which, as Pope Paul VI warned,

"can lead to a new and abusive form
of economic domination of the social, cultural,
and even political level."

A counterforce to such multinational corporations must be created:

there must arise a corresponding
multinational labor movement.

After a further agenda of unfinished business (twenty-one items for subsequent reflection!), the letter concludes with exhortations to offer responses to these suggestions, so that "solidarity with the oppressed" can begin.

Such emphases overlap our next area of concern, the need for the voiceless to gain a voice. But we must first note a danger in concentrating on liberation within the ecclesiastical community: such activity may create churches satisfied with ecclesiastical reform, losing sight of the fact that the *entire society* needs not just reform, but radical transformation. Nothing could please supporters of the *status quo* more than churches so turned in upon themselves that they ignore denunciation and annunciation toward an unjust society. The Appalachian letter is an important corrective to this temptation.

3. Hearing the Voice of the Voiceless

Our examples thus far have been domestic. But the church is a global community as well, and the example to which we now turn will offer that reminder.

Entering into "solidarity with the oppressed" must involve creating space in which the oppressed can both be heard and act on their own behalf. The voiceless need a voice. It is no longer enough to say that "the church must be the voice of the voiceless," speaking for those who cannot speak for themselves. The church must now be committed to "hearing the voice of the voiceless" and seeing to it that they can be heard *on their own terms.* Many will not listen to those who lack "appropriate" credentials: positions of power, savoir faire, items with which to bargain. "The remnant within the remnant" must ensure that the church becomes a place where the only credential necessary to gain a hearing is a cry of pain. Once that cry is heard within the church, the church must become the loudspeaker through which the cry can be transmitted elsewhere.

This will not be easy, for cries of pain indict us, as well as those beyond us. One test of the health of North American churches will be their ability to hear and respond to words of criticism from elsewhere in the world church. A specific test case is "An Open Letter to North American Christians," sent by thirteen Christian leaders from Latin America, at the time of the upcoming presidential election in the fall of 1976.[17] The letter gains in forcefulness with that event now behind us. It, too, deserves careful attention:

Our brothers and sisters:

. . . Can you comprehend the reason for our preoccupation [with your election]? . . . It is due to the fact that—with the exception of Cuba—we are trapped in the same system. We all move within one economic-political-military complex in which one finds committed [the] fabulous interests of the financial groups that dominate the life of your country and the creole oligarchies of our Latin American nations. Both groups, more allied today than ever, have held back time after time the great transformations that our people need and desperately demand.

If we still had some doubt regarding this sad and painful "Pan-American" reality, the scandalous intervention of the United States in the installation and maintenance of military regimes in Guatemala, Nicaragua, Brazil, Paraguay, Bolivia, etc.; the revelation of the activities of ITT and other North American businesses in Chile; the resounding case of Watergate; the discoveries [regarding the activities of] the CIA and other agencies of penetration and espionage in our countries; the shameful Panamanian enclave with its military training centers that our Christian and Latin American consciences cannot tolerate any longer . . .; all this and much more has been opening our eyes to a reality that . . . has demolished the image of "the great democracy of the North," which we have been taught to admire. . . .

Today, we Latin Americans are discovering that, apart from our own weaknesses and sins, not a few of our misfortunes, miseries and frustrations flow from and are perpetuated within a system that produces substantial benefits for your country but goes on swallowing us more and more in oppression, in impotence, in death. In a few words: your precious "American Way of Life"—the opulence of your magnates, your economic and military dominion—feeds in no small proportion on the blood that gushes, according to one of our most brilliant essayists, "from the open veins of Latin America."

The writers describe the regimes of terror in Latin America that are supported by the United States; the methods of electronic torture learned from us; the "silent genocide," i.e., starvation, to which economic exploitation condemns their people; the prisons, the corpses. They continue:

All this, our brothers and sisters, is carried out in the name of "democracy," in the name of "Western Christian civilization," on the backs of our people and with the benediction and the support of your government, of your armed forces, without which our dictators could not maintain themselves in power for much time.

Friends and fellow Christians, it is time that you realize that our continent is becoming one gigantic prison, and in some regions one vast cemetery: that human rights, the grand guidelines of the Gospel, are becoming a dead letter, without force. And all this in order to maintain a system, a structure of dependency, that benefits the mighty privileged persons of a minority of your land and of our land at the expense of the poor millions who are increasing throughout the width and breadth of the continent. . . . This letter seeks to be an anguished, fervent call to your conscience and to your responsibility as Christians.

The writers then spell out our "responsibility as Christians":

If in the past you felt it to be your apostolic duty to send us missionaries and economic resources, today the frontier of your witness and Christian solidarity is within your own country. The conscious, intelligent and responsible use of your vote, the appeal to your representatives in Congress, and the application of pressure by various means on your authorities can contribute to changing the course of our governments toward paths of greater justice and brotherhood or to accentuating a colonialist and oppressive policy over our peoples. In this sense you must ask yourselves if you will or will not be "your brother's keeper" in these lands of America, from which the blood of millions of Abels is clamoring to heaven.

We, between tears and groans, are interceding for you in order that you may respond with faithfulness to the historic responsibility that as citizens of one of the great contemporary powers and as disciples of Jesus Christ it falls on you to assume.

Can such passionate and powerful words be "heard" in North American churches? Reading the document to middle-class congregations produces reactions that run the gamut from anger, resentment, and defensiveness, to openness, acceptance, and shame. Some wonder if it is not an illicit mixing of religion and politics, others insist that it is only a clever bit of Marxist propaganda, and a few (the remnant within the remnant) acknowledge it as a disturbing statement of how things really are. The latter acknowledge that the denunciation-annunciation must force them into political activity, along the lines suggested by the closing paragraphs.

Taking our cue from the letter, we can ask what kind of political involvement would be appropriate in North America.

4. Taking Sides . . . Politically

Two presuppositions govern those brief comments about the political implications of liberation theology for us. The first is a reminder that we implicitly take sides all the time; lack of "political involvement" is actually political support of the *status quo*. Pressing for overt political commitment forces us to come clean about whether we are for change or for keeping things as they are. The second presupposition is that the case for the political involvement by Christians need not be argued here. The gospel of love forces us to act on behalf of those in need or, better, to find ways in which those in need can act on their own behalf. If such things are not yet clear, nothing that could be said now will be persuasive. What follows?

1. Recognizing that we have already "taken sides," liberation theology suggests that we are probably on the wrong side; in the terminology of Chapter 3 we are serving in Pharaoh's court. Our money, influence, jobs, life-styles, and political engagements support the present social-political-economic system. This system works effectively for us, but it does so at unacceptable costs to the majority of the human family, who are powerless to control their destiny and are victims of the "silent genocide" that actively contributes to the deaths of millions and the loss of hope for millions more. We do not actively will this and we probably deplore it heartily, but that does not change the reality of what happens.

2. If we really are on the wrong side, then our task is to change sides. This is the hardest part of all, since such a decision would be costly. It calls for *conversion*, for turning around, for seeing things from a new perspective, for saying "no" to many things and ideas we have held dear. We will speak briefly of conversion in the following section and note here only that a change of politics clearly involves a change of outlook, so that we assign a higher priority to others' right to live than we previously assigned to our own right to live affluently.

3. We soon discover that "human" concerns are also "political" concerns. Example: no person with any humane compassion can countenance the torture of political prisoners—burning, electric shock to the genitals, near-drowning, beating, torturing one person in the presence of another. Simply on a "human" level, quite apart from "political considerations," one has to seek to end such practices. But political considerations are already present. In Latin-American countries, for example, regimes that engage in such torture are dependent on the United States for the economic assistance that keeps them in power; dependent on the United States for the military hardware that discourages uprisings against them; dependent in many cases on U.S. corporations for the computers that enable them to track down political suspects; dependent in some cases on U.S. police academies for the training of the torturers. We not only condone torture, we sponsor it.

So what appears to be a "human" issue turns out to be a "political" issue as well. If we wish to stop the torture, we have to put pressure on our government to put pressure on other governments to stop such actions or face an end to arms shipments, an end to economic aid, an end to police training. We will be effective humanitarians only if we are effective politicians.

This happens on other "human" levels as well. We noted earlier that human rights involve not only *individual* rights but *social* rights as well—the right to jobs, education, health care, food, and housing. Here too, "human" concerns become political concerns. Getting food to starving people is not just a matter of private charity, but a complicated political exercise. Even more basic is a recognition that there is something wrong with a system of human exchange of goods that allows people to starve when there is food enough for all. To separate "human" and "political" concerns is to look at consequences rather than causes: we see the *consequence* of starving people and our instinct is to feed them and thus "put an end to starvation." But starvation will continue as long as the *causes* that bring it about are left unchallenged, for example, a system that increases rather than decreases the gap between rich and poor.

4. If "human" issues are in fact "political" issues, how do we act

politically to create a more humane world? Let us examine two alternatives that North American Christians, trying to cope with liberation themes, have been pondering:

Most opt for political *reformism*. They argue that the system under which we live has brought enormous material benefits to some and that there is no reason why its productivity cannot be extended so that those benefits are made available to all. The thing to do, therefore, is to work within that system, excise its crudities, enforce its strengths, and by education, enlightened political pressure, and hard work create a better life for all. With sufficient dedication and a willingness to learn from past mistakes, we can move in ways beneficial to all and not just to some. This is done by entering the electoral process and thereby humanizing structures that have often been dehumanizing in the past.

The problem with this approach is whether it can really meet the legitimate needs of "the wretched of the earth." Those who benefit from the present system are unwilling to have the system challenged at any *basic* level. They will not permit widespread redistribution of the wealth and goods of the world, for example, since that would threaten their ability to keep control. The system allows (in Herbert Marcuse's phrase) a measure of "repressive tolerance," i.e., protest and movement for change (that is its "tolerance"), but only protest and movement for change *up to a point* (that is its "repressiveness") —and that point is the point at which the powerless gain enough power to make a difference. Enough will be granted to defuse attempts to seek more; things can get a little better for some, but not much better for all.

Frustration with the possibility of significant change by reformism leads a few people to explore a second option, the option of *revolution*, the need to get rid of a competitive system that rewards a few at the cost of destroying many. Revolution proposes a basic restructuring of how we produce and distribute the earth's resources. The restructuring can have many names—the one most widely espoused in Third World countries is "socialism," in which the means of production are not in the hands of a few but under the control of the many. Since those now in control will not surrender control voluntarily, revolution involves some kind of taking of control. This need not mean physical violence—an important consideration in a discussion that usually equates revolution and bloodshed. The "revolution" for socialism in Chile, for example, was not won on the battlefield but in the polling booth; Allende's victory was achieved by the pushing of pens rather than the pulling of triggers. The "violence" in Chile was both the unjust situation that Allende sought to replace, and the military coup by which he was overthrown three years later, through an unconstitutional seizing of power by a military junta that had the support of U.S. Government and business interests.

It is curious that in a nation whose own history is based on "revolution" (and a violent one at that), there should be such fear even of the discussion of the viability of revolution or of a socialist alternative. It does not seem possible to reread the Bible (as liberation theologians have helped us to do) without entertaining the possibility of some sort of socialism (whether we call it that or not) and speculating about how it would be achieved.

Obviously, such a change would be brought about through a new kind of engagement in the political process; it would be romantic as well as unrealistic to anticipate an "overthrow" along the lines of most Third World coups. Whether those dedicated to such change seek to work through one of the major political parties or to develop a third party, whether changes should be sought first through local experiments or on the national level, how leadership and support could be enlisted, how a rhetoric could be developed that is persuasive rather than counterproductive—these and a host of other questions need exploration by "the remnant within the remnant."

Truly to hear what liberation theology says about the plight of the oppressed and our complicity in the continuation of that plight denies us the right to ongoing acceptance of things as they are, or to accepting token changes as a sufficient response. Our own inordinate power must be challenged, and we must organize politically to achieve that difficult end. This will demand a theology appropriate to our situation, and we now turn to a brief "preview" of what it might be like.

5. A Theology of "Letting Go"

We have been insisting *(a)* that theology must emerge out of the context of the theologizers rather than being imposed on them from elsewhere and *(b)* that *our* task is not to imitate theologies from Third World situations but to develop an indigenous theology for our situation. A significant attempt to do this has recently been made by Sr. Marie Augusta Neal, in *A Socio-Theology of Letting Go: The Role of a First World Church Facing Third World Peoples,* and we can be helped by summarizing some of her concerns:[18]

The reality of today's world is that the poor are rising up to claim what is rightfully theirs. This is a fact. We can deny the fact, or we can stop the poor, or we can recognize that "the task is to hear them and to take them seriously" (p. 42).

The theology of liberation grows out of this situation and affirms that the demands of the poor are right: "The Gospel mandates the poor to take what is theirs. . . . People have a right to the disposal of the resources of the land where they live" (p. 105). The gospel proclaims that "no right of ownership supercedes human need. . . . We know clearly that no matter who possesses food it belongs to hungry peoples" (p. 105). Consequently, "The Church is called upon to support the poor as they reach out to take what is rightfully theirs" (p. 2).

The church has a long record of failing to support the poor. Even when it has been sensitive, it often tries to act *for* the poor rather than *with* them. This becomes a new form of deception; those with a stake in the decision-making must be present, for "the fact is that no people can speak another's truth" (p. 74). If the poor are not involved in decision-making, it is axiomatic that the decisions will go against them rather than for them.

To escape this dilemma not only involves including the poor in decision-making but involves radical conversion of the nonpoor. It is not sufficient to patch up the effects of poverty.

Today we are called to a new approach to an age-old problem. It is a call
to work on eliminating the causes of poverty rather than merely alleviating
its results. This stance makes unambiguous what was unambiguous in
Gospel days, that is, that the interests of the poor have primacy in Christian service. Conversion consists in taking this step to change our allegiance and to choose this stance. This is the issue around which there is
polarization in the churches, between those who would perpetuate and
those who would eliminate the institutions that cause poverty. (P. 89)

Conversion and repentance, often associated with "spiritual" change,
have for Sr. Marie Augusta, a material and specific immediacy. Noting the passage (Luke 3:1–11) where John the Baptist spells out the
injunction "Bear fruits that befit repentance," by saying, "he who has
two coats, let him share with him who has none; and he who has food,
let him do likewise," she comments:

> This clearly indicates that repentance is directly associated with restoring
> goods to the poor. Sin, accordingly, must be associated with retaining
> goods that the poor need for their survival. (P. 107)

Conversion means looking at things from a different perspective
because one has been "turned around." If we look at the world from
the perspective that it is *working well for us,* we simply try to preserve
it as it is. If we see that the world needs *reform,* we try to make the
present system work better by education and other persuasive means.
But if we see that the systems *won't work anymore,* we move toward
more radical social change. "We will do this when we discover that
by keeping the rules we have devised, people suffer. . . . We will be
ready to relinquish our hold on the system. When the poor reach out
for what is theirs, we will be less likely to resist" (p. 15). Sr. Marie
Augusta is not suggesting that this will happen painlessly. But *a
theology of relinquishment, of diminishment, of "letting go"* is unavoidable if the nonpoor are to read the signs of the times realistically.

> A theology of liberation without a theology of relinquishment cannot
> touch us where we live and work, and so can change neither our lives nor
> the world in which we struggle. (P. 2)
> What is called for on the part of the non-poor is relinquishment.
> . . . Today, with the growing affirmation of a theology of liberation of the

poor, we need a corresponding method, peculiar to the non-poor, to think about God. . . When the poor rise to claim what belongs to them, as they are now doing, we need to know what the Gospel directs the non-poor to do. (Pp. 104–105)

Diminishment does not mean only personal acts of self-sacrifice. Sr. Marie Augusta stresses the social, structural dimension of relinquishment. "Relinquishment refers not to symbolic private acts but to public initiatives in the form of debt moratoria and the release of resources" (p. 2). Our *public* life must be challenged—the right to exact the last cent from poor countries who have hopelessly mortgaged their futures to us, or the right to hoard resources we do not need now but can sell later for a higher price if we keep them scarce. "This is a larger task than can be accomplished with private charity. It is a task of public planning" (p. 107).

A Socio-Theology of Letting Go provides a disturbing but unavoidable challenge to the nonpoor. It is not possible to take liberation theology seriously without drastic changes in *(a)* our own personal life-styles and *(b)* the corporate perspectives of business and government that must be held accountable to increasingly higher demands of social justice. Let us concede that diminishment in our own manner of living will chiefly produce new levels of personal conscientization, rather than "turning the system around," for the system is able to tolerate a significant number of unenthusiastic members. But this concession must not be used to evade the need for more modest standards of living, spending, accumulating, and wasting. Such things not only keep us alert but in time might have a cumulative aspect. Beyond this individual "letting go," however, there is need to find adroit and clever ways of challenging a system that allows a few in the world to have so much at the expense of the many, so that our nation will not only grasp less of the world's resources and share them with those in need, but will also look for better systems that do not allow inequities to build up so easily. This involves building up pressure (along the lines developed in our previous section), and being "wise as serpents and harmless as doves," which in our modern idiom means being politically savvy.

In addition to denunciations, we must search for annunciations in the form of individual and corporate alternatives, recognizing that small beginnings are the only way large movements ever get started. "The remnant within the remnant" might make its portion of the church one such alternative—a place in which, because people were not totally alone, they might risk more together than they would risk singly.

TWO CHEERS FOR THE CHURCH

If we move in the ways suggested above, we will discover that the size of "the remnant within the remnant" may shrink. So community will be even more important than before, both as a means of getting anything done, and also as a means of support. Does the Christian community offer such possibilities? Can "the remnant within the remnant" give at least two cheers for the church?

First Cheer: Liturgy Can Be Enabling

The first cheer we can give is a recognition that the church provides unexpected resources in its liturgical life.[19] Such a statement may seem counter to Miranda's concern in *Marx and the Bible* that the God of the Bible wants justice rather than cultus, and that there will be time for worship once justice has been achieved. Here, however, we will use "liturgy" in its widest (and original) sense, as "the people's work," meaning not only the work they do "in church" but the work they do wherever they are, so that the struggle for justice can itself be a "liturgical" act—a means by which praise is given to God.

In our previous linking of Jeremiah 22, Jeremiah 31, and the New Testament passages dealing with the Lord's Supper, we had a foretaste of this. These passages respectively insist that *(a)* to know God is to do justice, *(b)* knowing God is the content of the "new covenant" which thus embodies the doing of justice, and *(c)* the act of Jesus' self-giving prefigured in the eucharistic meal and fulfilled on the cross is the point at which these anticipations converge as a present reality. So to share the cup around the table of the Lord becomes an act of political commitment to the doing of justice rather than a retreat from a world where injustice is rampant.

This is enabling rather than evasive because it affirms that to enlist in the struggle for justice is not to go *against* the way things are meant to be, but to be aligned *with* the way things are meant to be. "To do justice" may place one in a minority position in society, but it is the place where the presence of God is located, and where one can therefore take heart rather than languish. The place where Christ is present is the place where bread is broken, which means the place where bodies are broken; the place where Christ is present is the place where wine is poured, which means the place where blood is shed, where life itself is being poured out. Today, bodies are being broken and blood is being shed in Chilean *poblaciones*, in Harlem apartments, in acts of deception between husbands and wives, in decisions made by boards of directors that continue "silent genocide" against the poor— there is no place where the reality of bread broken and wine poured is not paralleled by bodies broken and blood shed. The Eucharist affirms the "real presence" of Christ, not exclusively at a Communion table but in all the places to which that act around the table inextricably links us.

An episode is a better illustration than an essay:

Early in 1972 the First Presbyterian Church and St. Anne's Roman Catholic Church in Palo Alto, California, agreed to give "sanctuary" to any Vietnam veterans who found that they could no longer in conscience serve in the Armed Forces and wanted to declare that fact from within a church, forcing the military police to invade the sanctuary to take them prisoner.

The time came when a young man from the U.S. Navy, Rick Larson, approached the church. He had been on an aircraft carrier off the coast of Vietnam. It gradually came to him that those airplanes were taking off around the clock, and that Vietnamese peasants were therefore being destroyed around the clock. This became morally intolerable to him. So after some days in discussion with members of the congregation Rick surfaced in the Presbyterian church and announced that he would not return to his Navy duties.

He remained for several days and nights until his arrest, which took place in St. Anne's sanctuary to which the location was changed in mid-course.

During those days and nights in the church building, some significant things happened. Members of the churches, as well as people from the community, stayed with Rick to indicate their support and their willingness to be implicated in any legal action the government might later initiate. A new kind of community developed. People brought food inside the church, since Rick could not go outside the church. Where was the food to be placed? Where else but on the table already provided for the distribution of food? The Lord's table became a dining table from which full meals, and not just symbolic meals, were distributed. As bread and wine were dispensed from the Lord's table in many forms, it became increasingly hard to tell the difference between the so-called liturgical meals and the ordinary meals. A Eucharist invested a regular meal with new meaning. A regular meal gave a Eucharist new relevance. The breaking of bodies and the shedding of blood were what Rick wanted to avoid in Vietnam, and here were people celebrating a broken body and shed blood that were the seal of a promise that people need not break bodies and shed blood anymore.

At night, people slept on the pews and on the floor. There were songs into the wee small hours. Joan Baez appeared on two evenings, the new counterpart of the volunteer choir director. Clean-up crews emerged spontaneously. Rick's parents (a truck dispatcher and a woman ex-Marine) came from Detroit, not having been in a church for twenty years, and wept in gratitude for the support-community they found gathered around their son.

It was, for a few days, the world as it ought to be—a place where people were united around common concerns for which they were willing to put something on the line, a place where there was no such thing as a stranger, a place where there was food for all (where "he who had no money could come, buy and eat"), a place where concern for the other seemed to eclipse concern for the self.

It didn't last, of course. The MP's finally came, grim-faced and a little flustered, to embody law in a place where grace was clearly higher than law. Rick was taken to the nearby Navy brig, but the community stood behind him, and a few weeks later the Navy gave him the honorable discharge he had not expected to receive.[20]

The surest way for Christians to draw together a world that is improperly split into "spiritual" and "material" is to realize that the liturgy of the Lord's Supper invalidates such a split. The most "spiritual" claim possible (that God incarnate in Jesus Christ is present) is affirmed in the most "materialistic" way possible (eating and drinking). The risen Christ enters not into souls but into digestive tracts. There could be no stronger affirmation that the body is of concern to God, there could be no more rude denial of a "spiritualized" gospel.

Since food is shared around this table, it is also to be shared around other tables. Perhaps Paul's cryptic reference to "eating and drinking unto damnation" focuses on the hypocrisy, and therefore the damnable nature, of accepting food at this table while remaining unconcerned at the lack of food on other tables. To know God is to do justice.

The theme is present in other aspects of liturgical life. Let us recall the indictment of the rich and powerful, to which we have referred several times:

> [God] has scattered the proud in the imagination
>   of their hearts,
> he has put down the mighty from their thrones,
> and exalted those of low degree;
> he has filled the hungry with good things,
> and the rich he has sent empty away.
>   (Luke 1:51–53)

If we did not know the context of those words, we would probably conclude that they were:

a. spoken at a rally to enlist support for revolutionary activity,
b. part of a song with which the poor marched on the palace,
c. a paragraph from a leftist Zealot tract advocating overthrow of the existing order, or
d. all of the above.

Actually, the words are *part of a prayer*, Mary's act of devotion, as she sits with Elizabeth and they meditate on the forthcoming termination of their pregnancies. In Biblical experience, there is no way to isolate so-called acts of the spirit (praying, worshiping, singing) from the concern for justice set forth in the above lines.

Second Cheer: The Global Family Already Exists

We earlier heard Dom Helder Câmara speak of the "marvelous discovery" of those "all over the world, among all races, languages, religions, ideologies, who are committed to the struggle for love and justice."[21]

Our second cheer for the church is a footnote to that. We discover, in an era when global community is essential to human survival, that the global community already exists. Often to our surprise, we find the global community within the church, or, more accurately, within "the remnant of the remnant" that constitutes the hope of the church.

Let us illustrate by returning to the "Open Letter to North American Christians." The places where that document most deeply threatens us are the places where we think of ourselves chiefly as U.S. citizens, as white persons, as members of a privileged class, and as parts of an institutional church that has been acquiescent in the evils the letter indicts. It follows that if our first loyalty is to the United States, we will resist the notion that our nation is a predator; if our first loyalty is to our white skin, we will resist the notion that whites have been ripping off nonwhites; if our first loyalty is to our class, we will resist the notion that it is on the side of repression and destruction; if our first loyalty is to the institutional church, we will resist the notion that it is deeply complicit in the evil deeds that darken our world today. All such loyalties are too parochial, too partial. They must be shattered, for they in turn are shattering human hopes everywhere. We need a wider loyalty.

Every now and then this community with a wider loyalty surfaces —fragmentarily, tremblingly, sometimes courageously, an amazing network that might be called "God's underground." We sense this when we listen to a Helder Câmara, or derive hope from a Martin

Luther King, or affirm a Pope John, or receive an "Open Letter to North American Christians," or give thanks for an Abraham Heschel, or hear that Beyers Naudé has been banned for saying "no" to the South African government, or have our political complacency challenged by a César Chavez, or learn about hope from a Beatriz Couch. We confront the countless nameless ones, whether in prison in South Korea, or working in Lima, or teaching in Bangalore, or struggling in Cape Town, those who put themselves on the line in ways we never come close to doing. We discover that there already is a "cloud of witnesses," and that we are part of that band, however lacking in courage we may be.

The global community does not have to be created. It already is. It may be feeble, it may be hard to see, but we have a promise on high authority that the gates of hell will not prevail against it. It is the community in which we rediscover that the meal around a common table is not simply a symbol of human community, but an expression of the divine-human community through which we are strengthened to look in directions we have feared to look, and walk in ways we have feared to walk; in which we rediscover that the scenario for our own future is too threatening to entertain unless that future is also God's future; in which we rediscover that the daily resources of forgiveness and mercy are essential ingredients in struggling for human justice against odds that otherwise would seem overwhelming. From such rediscovery we can set ourselves to embody a global community grounded in the conviction that God is the God of all persons, a God who has sent Jesus Christ so that all may have life and have it more abundantly—no one excepted, everyone accepted. Then we may begin to know what Paul meant when he said about Jesus Christ that "in him all things hold together" (Col. 1:17).

The Last Word: The Primacy of Act

Many words have been written and spoken about liberation theology. They can be a trap, for there is all the difference in the world between talking about acts of liberation and engaging in liberating acts.

As a reminder of this danger, we will give the last word to Gustavo

188 *Theology in a New Key*

Gutiérrez, whose own life has been an acting out of "solidarity with the oppressed" along with rigorous scholarly commitment. Concluding his survey of the "political theology" of continental Roman Catholicism, the "theology of hope" of continental Protestantism, the "theology of revolution" found in both Latin America and Europe, as well as the "theology of liberation" to which he and his friends are committed, he writes:

> All the political theologies, the theologies of hope, of revolution, and of liberation, are not worth one genuine act of solidarity with exploited social classes. They are not worth one act of faith, love and hope committed—in whatever manner—in active participation to liberate human beings from all that dehumanizes them and prevents them from living according to the will of God.[22]

Notes

Chapter 1. ESTABLISHED HARMONIES:
A DIMINISHED SEVENTH IN NEED OF RESOLUTION

1. Cf. *U.S. News & World Report*, April 11, 1977, pp. 55, 58.

2. Elie Wiesel, *The Oath* (Random House, Inc., 1973), p. 214.

3. See not only Gustavo Gutiérrez, *A Theology of Liberation*, but also his long essay *Teología Desde el Reverso de la Historia*, portions of which are included in Sergio Torres and Virginia Fabella (eds.), *The Emergent Gospel*.

4. References below are to the paragraph numbers common to various editions of the encyclicals.

5. *Gaudium et Spes*, para. 69, translation modified to eliminate sexist language.

6. Hugo Assmann, *Theology for a Nomad Church*, p. 63.

7. *Populorum Progressio*, Part I, para. 26.

8. *Octogesima Adveniens*, para. 31.

9. Marie Augusta Neal, *A Socio-Theology of Letting Go: The Role of a First World Church Facing Third World Peoples*, p. 63.

10. Historical material and bibliography can be found in my book *The Ecumenical Revolution*, rev. and enlarged ed. (Doubleday & Company, Inc., Anchor Books, 1969).

11. Useful interpretive resources are Edward Duff, *The Social Thought of the World Council of Churches* (Association Press, 1956), carrying the story up through the Evanston Assembly of 1954, and Paul Bock, *In Search of a Responsible World Society: The Social Teachings of the World Council of Churches* (The Westminster Press, 1974), covering the entire history topically.

12. W. A. Visser 't Hooft (ed.), *The First Assembly of the World Council*

12. W. A. Visser 't Hooft (ed.), *The First Assembly of the World Council of Churches* (Harper & Brothers, 1949), p. 80. The following citation is from this source.

13. Cf. John W. Turnbull (ed.), *Ecumenical Documents on Church and Society, 1925–1953* (Geneva: World Council of Churches, 1954), pp. 143–152. Subsequent citations are from this source.

14. W. A. Visser 't Hooft (ed.), *The Evanston Report* (London: SCM Press, Ltd., 1955), p. 113. Subsequent citations are from this source.

15. W. A. Visser 't Hooft (ed.), *The New Delhi Report* (Association Press, 1962), esp. pp. 94–99.

16. Paul Abrecht and M. M. Thomas (eds.), *World Conference on Church and Society* (Geneva: World Council of Churches, 1967), p. 18. Subsequent citations are from this source.

17. Cf. Norman Goodall (ed.), *The Uppsala Report* (Geneva: World Council of Churches, 1968), p. 48. Subsequent citations are from this source.

18. *World Development: The Challenge to the Churches* (Geneva: Exploratory Committee on Society, Development, and Peace, 1969), p. 20. Subsequent citations are from this source.

19. C. I. Itty, "Are We Yet Awake? The Development Debate Within the Ecumenical Movement," *The Ecumenical Review,* January 1974, pp. 6–20.

20. On these shifts, cf. also the detailed account by Carl-Henric Grenholm, *Christian Social Ethics in a Revolutionary Age* (Uppsala: Verbum, 1973), which is particularly helpful in describing the movement from a "theology of the responsible society" toward a "theology of revolution."

21. Emilio Castro, "Bangkok, The New Opportunity," *International Review of Missions,* April 1973, p. 139. Subsequent citations are from this source.

22. Cf. David Paton (ed.), *Breaking Barriers: Nairobi 1975* (Wm. B. Eerdmans Publishing Company, 1976), pp. 41–57. Subsequent citations are from this source.

23. An excellent assessment of the first five years of the Program to Combat Racism is found in Elisabeth Adler, *A Small Beginning* (Geneva: World Council of Churches, 1974).

Chapter 2. A Challenge to the Established Harmonies: "The View from Below"

1. Information about Fr. Camilo Torres can be found in John Gerassi (ed.), *Revolutionary Priest: The Complete Writings and Messages of Camilo Torres,* and German Guzman, *Camilo Torres* (Sheed & Ward, Inc., 1969).

2. The full texts from Medellín are available in English in *The Church in*

the Present-Day Transformation of Latin America in the Light of the Council, Vol. II: Conclusions, available through the United States Catholic Conference, Washington, D.C., 1970. For the texts on "Justice" and "Poverty in the Church," cf. Between Honesty and Hope. For the texts on "Justice" and "Peace," cf. David J. O'Brien and Thomas A. Shannon (eds.), Renewing the Earth (Doubleday & Company, Inc., Image Books, 1977). Page numbers below are to the first work cited.

3. Cf. John Eagleson (ed.), Christians and Socialism, for documents. Two books in Spanish provide additional material: Hugo Assmann et al., Cristianos por el Socialismo: Exigencias de una Opción (Montevideo: Tierra Nueva, 1973), and Pablo Richard, Cristianos por el Socialismo: Historia y Documentación.

4. These and other contrasts are drawn by Guilio Girardi in Assmann et al., op. cit., pp. 68–70.

5. Cf. Eagleson (ed.), op. cit., pp. 179–228, for the text of the hierarchy's statement (which does not represent one of the great moments of episcopal insight), along with a response by Gonzalo Arroyo, S.J., pp. 229–246.

6. Eagleson (ed.), op. cit., pp. 160–175. Page references below are to this source. The chief drafters were Guilio Girardi, who was cited in note 4, above, Hugo Assmann and Gustavo Gutiérrez, who will be cited many times below, and Pablo Richard, whose book, cited in note 3, above, is a valuable reference work.

7. Helder Câmara, The Desert Is Fertile, pp. 27–28.

8. Frederick Herzog, Liberation Theology, p. 258.

9. Cf. Sergio Torres and John Eagleson (eds.), Theology in the Americas, p. 278, slightly edited.

10. For impetus in developing these differentations, I am indebted to Gregory Baum.

11. Two recent books that are helpful on these questions are José Miguez-Bonino, Christians and Marxists, written out of the Latin-American situation, and Jan Lochman, Encountering Marx (Fortress Press, 1977), written out of the situation in Eastern Europe.

12. Cf. further Gutiérrez, A Theology of Liberation, esp. pp. 84–88. Assmann, Theology for a Nomad Church, uses the concept of dependency as a normative theme.

13. Gutiérrez, A Theology of Liberation, p. 275. Quotations are used by permission of Orbis Books.

14. Cf. the helpful discussion in Paulo Freire, Pedagogy of the Oppressed.

15. From the song "When the Changes Come" (1968), by Al Carmines.

16. Gustavo Gutiérrez, in The Witness, April 1977, p. 5, from which much of the present discussion has been paraphrased.

17. Gregory Baum, in Torres and Eagleson (eds.), op. cit., p. 407.

18. Ibid., p. 311.

19. Cf. *inter alia*, Gutiérrez, *A Theology of Liberation*, esp. pp. 36–37, and 176ff., from which much of the above discussion is drawn.

Chapter 3. The Melodic Stridency of Scripture: Marx, Luke, and John

1. Juan Luis Segundo, *The Liberation of Theology*, p. 102.
2. Karl Mannheim, *Ideology and Utopia* (Harcourt, Brace and Company, Inc., 1936), p. 40, italics added.
3. Gutiérrez, *A Theology of Liberation*, pp. 235, 249.
4. Luke 4:18–19, paraphrasing Isa. 61:1–2; cf. also Ps. 146.
5. William Manson, *The Gospel of Luke* (Harper & Brothers, n.d.), pp. 41–42.
6. *The Interpreter's Bible*, Vol. 8 (Abingdon-Cokesbury Press, 1952), p. 92.
7. Manson, *op. cit.*, p. 12, italics added.
8. *Ibid.*, p. 65, italics added.
9. José Miguez-Bonino, *Doing Theology in a Revolutionary Situation*, p. 102.
10. Gustavo Gutiérrez, *Praxis of Liberation and Human Faith*, p. 44, modified to avoid sexist language. Cf. also Segundo, *op. cit.*, Ch. 1.
11. Beatriz Melano Couch, in Torres and Eagleson (eds.), *Theology in the Americas*, pp. 305–306.
12. *Ibid.*, p. 306.
13. The following material is drawn chiefly from Assmann, *Theology for a Nomad Church;* Ernesto Cardenal, *The Gospel in Solentiname;* Ignacio Ellacuria, *Freedom Made Flesh;* Alfredo Fierro, *The Militant Gospel;* Enzo Gatti, *Rich Church—Poor Church?* (1974); Gutiérrez, *A Theology of Liberation;* José P. Miranda, *Marx and the Bible* and *Being and the Messiah;* Segundo, *The Liberation of Theology*. All published by Orbis Books.
14. Jer. 22:13–16, using the translation in Miranda, *Marx and the Bible*, p. 44.
15. Gerassi (ed.), *Revolutionary Priest*, pp. 368–369, citation altered to avoid sexist language. The Scriptural reference is to Matt. 5:23–24.
16. Gutiérrez, *A Theology of Liberation*, pp. 201-202, modified to avoid sexist language.
17. Lochman, *Encountering Marx*, p. 98.

Chapter 4. Chords of Discord: A Twelve-Tone Scale of Sorts

1. Cf. Segundo, *The Liberation of Theology*, p. 234.
2. *Ibid.*, pp. 136–138, for an elaboration of these points, and Peter Wag-

ner, *Latin American Theology, in toto.* A more balanced critique from an "evangelical" perspective is Orlando E. Costas, *The Church and Its Mission.*

3. Cf., for example, the argument of the Chilean bishops condemning Christians for Socialism, in Eagleson (ed.), *Christians and Socialism,* pp. 179–228.

4. René de Visme Williamson, "The Theology of Liberation," *Christianity Today,* Aug. 8, 1975, pp. 7–13. Subsequent citations are from this source.

5. Michael Novak, "Theology of Liberation," *National Catholic Reporter,* Nov. 21, 1975.

6. David Tracy, *Blessed Rage for Order* (The Seabury Press, Inc., 1975), p. 242.

7. Cf. Gutiérrez, *A Theology of Liberation,* pp. 149–153, for example.

8. Williamson, *loc. cit.,* p. 10.

9. Hans Küng, *On Being a Christian* (Doubleday & Company, Inc., 1976), p. 570. For a longer response to this and other statements of Küng about liberation theology, cf. my review in *Theology Today,* July 1977, pp. 205–211.

10. Peter Hodgson, *New Birth of Freedom* (Fortress Press, 1976).

11. Karl Barth, *Against the Stream,* ed. by Ronald Gregor Smith (Philosophical Library, Inc., 1954), p. 41.

12. Gordon Zahn, "The Bondage of Liberation: A Pacifist Reflection," *Worldview,* March 1977, pp. 20–24.

13. Denis Goulet, "Pyramids of Sacrifice: The High Price of Social Change," *Christianity and Crisis,* Oct. 13, 1975, p. 234.

14. I have elaborated the comments made above in *Religion and Violence* (The Westminster Press, 1973).

15. Gutiérrez, *A Theology of Liberation,* p. ix, italics added.

16. Miguez-Bonino, *Christians and Marxists,* p. 7. Such forthrightness makes particularly unfortunate Stephen Neill's characterization of Miguez-Bonino as one who "accepts hook, line and sinker the Marxist analysis of society" (Stephen Neill, *Salvation Tomorrow,* p. 82; Abingdon Press, 1976)

17. Alejandro Cussianovich, *Desde los Pobres de la Tierra: Perspectivas de Vida Religiosa,* soon to be translated into English as *From the Poor of the Earth: Perspectives on the Religious Life* (Orbis Books).

18. *Ibid.,* p. 155, my translation.

19. For further information on this episode, cf. *Latinamerica Press,* Vol. 9, No. 8 (Feb. 24, 1977).

20. T. F. Torrance, "Dietetic Deficiencies the Church Can Cure," *Christianity Today,* Sept. 24, 1976, pp. 10–12.

21. John Howard Yoder, "Exodus and Exile: The Two Faces of Liberation," *Cross Currents,* 23 (1973), pp. 297–309.

22. It should be stressed that Latin-American theologians do far more than hover over only a few texts, or (as is frequently charged) deal almost

exclusively with the Old Testament. Miranda draws from the Bible as a whole, and his most recent work, *Being and the Messiah,* is a detailed study of liberation themes in the Fourth Gospel. The pioneer North American work, Herzog's *Liberation Theology,* is also an exegetical study of the Fourth Gospel. Gutiérrez's writings deal with a great variety of Biblical materials.

23. Cf. Eagleson (ed.), *op. cit.,* pp. 179–228.

24. Richard Neuhaus, "Liberation Theology and the Captivities of Jesus," *Worldview,* June 1973, pp. 41–48.

25. Beatriz Couch, in Torres and Eagleson (eds.), *Theology in the Americas,* p. 307, citation changed slightly, italics added.

26. The next paragraphs draw on portions of my article, "Context Affects Content," *Christianity and Crisis,* July 18, 1977, pp. 170–174.

27. Cf. Thomas Sanders, "The Theology of Liberation: Christian Utopianism," *Christianity and Crisis,* Sept. 17, 1973, pp. 167–173. In a later response (*Christianity and Crisis,* Nov. 26, 1973, pp. 249–251) Sanders modified his position, but his statement is still a useful presentation of a position widely held by others.

28. Gutiérrez, *A Theology of Liberation,* p. 238, italics added. This paragraph is also an adequate rebuttal to the reductionist critiques we have examined. Cf. also note 12, Ch. 6, below.

29. Freire, *Pedagogy of the Oppressed,* p. 28.

30. Fierro, *The Militant Gospel,* p. 364. Sequential citations are from this source.

31. Assmann, *Theology for a Nomad Church,* p. 129.

32. The following pages are indebted to Roberto Oliveros, *Liberación y Teología: Genesis y Crecimiento de una Reflexión, 1966–1976,* esp. pp. 317–329. Lopez Trujillo's position can be found in *Liberación: Diálogos en el CELAM* (Bogotá, 1974), pp. 27–67, and, more recently in English, *Liberation or Revolution? An Examination of the Priest's Role in the Socio-economic Struggle in Latin America* (Our Sunday Visitor, Inc., 1977).

33. Cf. Miguez-Bonino, *op. cit.,* esp. pp. 144–150, and Jürgen Moltmann, "An Open Letter to José Miguez-Bonino," *Christianity and Crisis,* March 29, 1975, pp. 57–63. Sequential citations are from these sources.

34. Miguez-Bonino, *op. cit.,* p. 148.

35. Moltmann, *loc. cit.,* p. 60.

36. Gutiérrez, *Teología Desde el Reverso de la Historia,* 59 pp.

37. Cf. "El Diálogo Teología Política, Teología de la Liberación," *Taller de Teología,* Vol. I, No. 1 (1976), a publication of the Comunidad Teológica de Mexico, Mexico City, from which the above comments are drawn.

Chapter 5. "How Shall We Sing the Lord's Song in a
Strange Land?":
Discovering the Word of God for Us

1. The previous three paragraphs are adapted from my essay in Torres and
Eagleson (eds.), *Theology in the Americas,* p. xiv.

2. In order that the musical metaphor not overwhelm the argument, we
shall here use "story" and "song" as equivalents.

3. Cf. further my *Is Faith Obsolete?* (The Westminster Press, 1974), esp.
pp. 56–58.

4. If space permitted, the point could be elaborated by the similar impingement of other domestic stories: Chicanos, Nisei, Poles, even Daughters of
the American Revolution.

5. Cf. "Has Latin America a Choice?" *America,* Feb. 22, 1969.

6. Helps in beginning this task are the early portions of George W. Forell
(ed.), *Christian Social Teachings* (Doubleday & Company, Inc., 1966), and
Ernst Troeltsch, *The Social Teachings of the Christian Churches* (London:
George Allen & Unwin, Ltd., 1931), Vol. I.

7. Useful resources are George H. Williams, *The Radical Reformation*
(The Westminster Press, 1962), and George H. Williams and Angel M.
Mergal (eds.), *Spiritual and Anabaptist Writers* (The Library of Christian
Classics, Vol. XXV), (The Westminster Press, 1957). Cf. also Lowell H.
Zuck (ed.), *Christianity and Revolution: Radical Christian Testimonies,
1520–1650* (Temple University Press, 1975); Michael L. Walzer, *The Revo-
lution of the Saints* (Harvard University Press, 1965); and Norman R. C.
Cohn, *The Pursuit of the Millennium* (Harper & Row Publishers, Inc.,
Torchbook, 1961).

8. John C. Bennett, "Fitting the Liberation Theme Into Our Theological
Agenda," *Christianity and Crisis,* July 18, 1977, p. 167.

9. Robert T. Handy (ed.), *The Social Gospel in America, 1870–1920*
(Oxford University Press, 1966), p. 308, introducing an essay by Walter
Rauschenbusch on "Dogmatic and Practical Socialism."

10. Walter Rauschenbusch, *A Theology for the Social Gospel* (The Mac-
millan Company, 1917), pp. 78, 79.

11. *Ibid.,* pp. 80–81, italics added.

12. Basic resources are Charles H. Hopkins, *The Rise of the Social Gospel
in American Protestantism, 1865–1915* (Yale University Press, 1940); Paul
A. Carter, *The Decline and Revival of the Social Gospel* (Cornell University
Press, 1956); Handy (ed.), *op. cit.,* with selections from Gladden, Ely, and
Rauschenbusch.

13. Cf. the recent biography by Wilhelm Pauck and Marion Pauck, *Paul*

Tillich: His Life and Thought, Vol. I: *Life* (Harper & Row, Publishers, Inc., 1976), esp. Ch. 3; Paul Tillich's own autobiographical reflections in *On the Boundary* (Charles Scribner's Sons, 1966), and his two volumes of early writings where the dialogue with Marxism and socialism is central: *Political Expectation* (Harper & Row, Publishers, Inc., 1971) and *The Socialist Decision* (Harper & Row, Publishers, Inc., 1977).

14. Cf. spectrum of viewpoints in George Hunsinger (ed.), *Karl Barth and Radical Politics* (The Westminster Press, 1976).

15. Karl Barth, *Church Dogmatics,* Vol. II, Part 1, ed. by G. W. Bromiley and T. F. Torrance (Edinburgh: T. & T. Clark, 1957), p. 386.

16. Barth, *Against the Stream,* p. 36.

17. Reference to Tillich and Barth does not exhaust the possibility of enrichment between liberation theology and other modern theological positions. Attention has been called to the exchange with Moltmann. Cf. also Burton Cooper, "How Does God Act in Our Time? An Invitation to a Dialogue Between Process and Liberation Theologies," in *Union Seminary Quarterly Review,* Fall 1976, pp. 25–35.

18. Cf. Robert N. Bellah, *The Broken Covenant* (The Seabury Press, Inc., 1975).

19. Cf. John Coleman, "Civil Religion and Liberation Theology," in Torres and Eagleson (eds.), *op. cit.,* pp. 129–130.

20. Joe Holland, *The American Journey.* Subsequent citations are from this source.

21. Thomas Ambrogi, in an unpublished paper, acknowledging dependence on Vaughan Hinton, of Action for World Development.

22. Basil Moore (ed.), *The Challenge of Black Theology in South Africa* (John Knox Press, 1974), p. 5, italics added.

23. James H. Cone, *A Black Theology of Liberation* (J. B. Lippincott Company, 1970), pp. 185–186.

24. Freire, *Pedagogy of the Oppressed,* p. 42.

25. Gutiérrez, *A Theology of Liberation,* p. 276.

26. Guilio Girardi, cited in *ibid.,* p. 285.

27. Freire, *Pedagogy of the Oppressed,* pp. 34–35.

28. Benjamin A. Reist, *Theology in Red, White, and Black,* pp. 183–184.

29. Cf. comments in Chapter 6, about the church as a possible community that can transcend nationalistic lines.

30. Cf. the further discussion of this issue in Chapter 6, below.

Chapter 6. Two Cheers for the Church:
A Not-Quite Hallelujah Chorus

1. My book *Frontiers for the Church Today* (Oxford University Press, 1973) spells out in more detail my own affirmations.

2. A possible model is provided by medieval religious "orders," where individuals, not forsaking the church as such, nevertheless banded together to undertake specific tasks the church as a whole was not ready to undertake. Cf. further *Frontiers for the Church Today*, pp. 97–101.

3. Joseph Ratzinger, *Le nouveau peuple de Dieu*, p. 228, my translation. Cf. further on the danger of the church representing only the "dominant people," Gutiérrez's section of Gustavo Gutiérrez and Richard Shaull, *Liberation and Change.*

4. Cf. Helder Câmara, *Spiral of Violence* and *The Desert Is Fertile*. I have developed some conclusions for today about "the Abrahamic minority" in *Is Faith Obsolete?* esp. pp. 137–146.

5. Câmara, *Spiral of Violence*, p. 69.

6. Câmara, *The Desert Is Fertile*, p. 3. Subsequent citations are from this source.

7. Jürgen Moltmann, "Christian Theology and Its Problems Today," *Theology Digest*, Winter 1971, pp. 308–317.

8. *The Church in the Present-Day Transformation of Latin America in the Light of the Council*, Vol. II: *Conclusions* (Bogotá: CELAM, 1970), p. 122, "Pastoral Care of the Masses."

9. Paulo Freire, "Education as Cultural Action: An Introduction," in L. Colonnese (ed.), *Conscientization for Liberation* (United States Catholic Conference, 1971), pp. 109–122. Cf. also Gutiérrez, *A Theology of Liberation*, pp. 114–116, 232–234, and 265–272.

10. Gutiérrez, *A Theology of Liberation*, p. 267.

11. *Ibid.*

12. *Ibid.*, p. 272. This quotation is important not only for what it affirms but as a further refutation of the charge that liberation theologians have an uncritical view of the perfectibility of human achievements in history.

13. *Ibid.*, p. 270.

14. Among the growing literature on liberation themes in feminist theology, cf. Rosemary Radford Ruether (ed.), *Religion and Sexism* (Simon & Schuster, Inc., 1974), for historical overview; Letty M. Russell, *Human Liberation in a Feminist Perspective—A Theology* (The Westminster Press, 1974), on relationships with Third World and black theology; and Sheila D. Collins, *A Different Heaven and Earth* (Judson Press, 1974); for a creative statement, cf. also Carol Christ, "The New Feminist Theology: A Review of the Literature," *Religious Studies Review*, October 1977, pp. 203–212.

15. Cf. further James H. Cone, *God of the Oppressed* (The Seabury Press, Inc., 1975), and *The Spirituals and the Blues* (The Seabury Press, Inc., 1973). For a historical treatment, cf. Gayraud S. Wilmore, *Black Religion and Black Radicalism* (Doubleday & Company, Inc., 1972).

16. "This Land Is Home to Me," written in blank verse, is available from the Catholic Committee of Appalachia, 31-A S. 3d Avenue, Prestonburg, Ky.

41653. Also reprinted in O'Brien and Shannon (eds.), *Renewing the Earth*, pp. 471–515.

17. "An Open Letter to North American Christians," *Christianity and Crisis*, Oct. 18, 1976, pp. 230–232. Copyright © 1976. Reprinted by permission of Christianity and Crisis, Inc.

18. Neal, *A Socio-Theology of Letting Go*. Page numbers are incorporated within the text below.

19. For a fuller treatment of the approach to liturgy presupposed here, cf. my *The Spirit of Protestantism* (Oxford University Press, 1961), Chs. 12 and 13, and *Frontiers for the Church Today*, Ch. 9.

20. The above paragraphs are adapted from "Community-making as Ministry," *NICM Journal*, January 1977, pp. 24–36.

21. Câmara, *The Desert Is Fertile*, p. 4.

22. Gutiérrez, *A Theology of Liberation*, p. 308, translation slightly altered to avoid sexist language. Cf. *Teología de la Liberación*, p. 388.

Annotated Bibliography

This bibliography is suggestive rather than exhaustive. The frustration entailed in cutting it to manageable size has been intense. Many books listed have bibliographies of their own, so readers can gain access to more material.

BASIC BIBLIOGRAPHICAL RESOURCES

Bibliografía Teológica Comentada del Área Iberoamericana. Buenos Aires: ISEDET, 1975.

An annotated bibliography in Spanish, covering all Latin-American literature dealing with Biblical and theological materials. An indispensable reference tool. Three volumes so far, covering material through 1975.

Vanderhoff, Frank. *Bibliography: Latin American Theology of Liberation.* Cuernavaca, Mexico: CIDOC. Doc. I/I 73/398.

Lists materials published through 1973.

HELPFUL INTRODUCTIONS

MacEoin, Gary. *Revolution Next Door: Latin America in the 1970's.* Holt, Rhinehart and Winston, Inc., 1971.

Historical and political background of the context of liberation theology.

Miguez-Bonino, José. *Doing Theology in a Revolutionary Situation.* Fortress Press, 1975.

An excellent map, overview, and reader's guide that helps make other books understandable. Good bibliography.

CORPORATE EXPRESSIONS FROM LATIN AMERICA

Anderson, Gerald H., and Stransky, Thomas F. (eds.). *Mission Trends No. 3: Third World Theologies.* Paulist Press, 1976.

Articles from Latin America, Asia, and Africa.

Colonnese, Louis M. (ed.). *Human Rights and the Liberation of Man in the Americas.* University of Notre Dame Press, 1970.
————. *Conscientization for Liberation.* United States Catholic Conference, 1971.

Papers from the Catholic Inter-American Cooperation Program conferences of 1970 and 1971; essays by Câmara, Gutiérrez, Freire, Segundo, and others.

Eagleson, John (ed.). *Christians and Socialism.* Orbis Books, 1975.

Account of the rise (and fall) of a group in Chile known as Christians for Socialism. A significant piece of history that highlights the pros and cons of Christian (and church) involvement in the politics of left, right, and center.

Geffré, Claude, and Gutiérrez, Gustavo (eds.). *The Mystical and Political Dimension of Christian Faith.* Concilium Series, The Seabury Press, Inc., 1974.

Excellent articles by excellent theologians, such as Gutiérrez, Boff, Comblin, Segundo, and Miguez-Bonino.

Latin American Episcopal Council (CELAM), *The Church in the Present-Day Transformation of Latin America in the Light of the Council.* Bogotá: General Secretariat of CELAM, 1970, Vol. II.

Texts of the sixteen documents of the Medellín Conference of 1968. Those on "Justice," "Peace," "Education," and "Poverty in the Church" are particularly useful.

Peruvian Bishops' Commission for Social Action (eds.). *Between Honesty and Hope.* Orbis Books, 1970.

Primary sources from Latin-American countries, dealing with poverty, violence, structural evil, church responsibility, and social justice. Includes excerpts from Medellín.

Books by Individual Latin-American Theologians

Alves, Reubem. *A Theology of Human Hope.* Corpus Books, 1969.

A pioneer work in Latin-American theology, helpful particularly in its critique of European theological models.

Assmann, Hugo. *Theology for a Nomad Church.* Orbis Books, 1976.

Four independent essays, the longest of which traces the development of liberation themes.

Câmara, Helder. *Spiral of Violence.* Dimension Books, 1971.

Particularly useful in distinguishing three forms of violence: injustice, revolt, and repression.

―――. *The Desert Is Fertile.* Orbis Books, 1974.

Meditations and poems containing social dynamite.

Cardenal, Ernesto. *The Gospel in Solentiname.* Orbis Books, 1976, 1978.

Each Sunday at Mass in Solentiname the gospel lesson is read and the people reflect together on the meaning of the Gospels when read from "the view from below." Two volumes now available.

Costas, Orlando E. *The Church and Its Mission: A Shattering Critique from the Third World.* Tyndale House Publishers, 1974.

Important contribution from an "evangelical" perspective, by one who is both appreciative and critical of liberation theology, and also critical of "evangelical" disengagement.

―――. *Theology of the Crossroads in Contemporary Latin America.* Amsterdam: Rodopi, 1976.

Detailed treatment of Protestant mission strategies from 1969 to 1974. Extensive bibliography.

Dussel, Enrique D. *History and the Theology of Liberation.* Orbis Books, 1976.
―――. *Ethics and the Theology of Liberation.* Orbis Books, 1978.

Essays by an important Latin-American historian.

Ellacuria, Ignacio. *Freedom Made Flesh: The Mission of Christ and His Church.* Orbis Books, 1976.

Assessing the political dimension of Jesus' mission, and the problem of violence in relation to the cross.

Freire, Paulo. *Pedagogy of the Oppressed.* The Seabury Press, Inc., 1972.

A seminal contribution to the view of education that predominates in most liberation thinking. Challenges educational methods that buttress the *status quo.* The prose style is difficult; the content makes the struggle worthwhile.

Gerassi, John (ed.). *Revolutionary Priest: The Complete Writings and Messages of Camilo Torres.* Vintage Books, Inc., 1971.

The chronological order of the essays enables one to trace Camilo's disengagement from gradualist means of social change.

Gutiérrez, Gustavo. *A Theology of Liberation.* Orbis Books, 1971.

The most important single work. Biblical rootage, and social analysis. Full documentation.

———. *Praxis of Liberation and Human Faith.* San Antonio, 1977.

Lectures providing a brief introduction to many of Gutiérrez's concerns.

Gutiérrez, Gustavo, and Shaull, Richard. *Liberation and Change.* John Knox Press, 1977.

Gutiérrez on "Freedom and Salvation: A Political Problem," and Shaull on "The Death and Resurrection of the American Dream." Gutiérrez's essay has historical material that supplements the conclusions arrived at in his other writings.

Illich, Ivan. *The Church, Change and Development.* Herder & Herder, 1970.

See especially "Yankee Go Home," an acerbic statement of why Yankee know-how and presence are not welcomed by many Latin Americans.

Miguez-Bonino, José. *Christians and Marxists.* Wm. B. Eerdmans Publishing Company, 1976.

Miguez-Bonino's Christian commitments stand out clearly, forcing the reader to grapple with why the author finds Marxism important for ongoing theological activity.

Miranda, José P. *Marx and the Bible.* Orbis Books, 1974.

Deals exegetically with the overall theme that "to know God is to do justice." An arsenal of material for those who confront charges that "religion and politics don't mix." Not much explicit Marx, but a great deal of Bible.

————. *Being and the Messiah: The Message of St. John.* Orbis Books, 1977.

The relation of the Johannine literature to liberation themes, leavened with insights from Marx.

Segundo, Juan Luis. *The Liberation of Theology.* Orbis Books, 1976.

Contends that the important thing about liberation theology is not its content but its method. A serious challenge to earlier ways of doing theology.

Sobrino, Jon. *Christology at the Crossroads: A Latin American Approach.* Orbis Books, 1978.

A major work offering "a Christology that is historically positioned and constructed from the Latin-American situation of oppression, injustice, and exploitation."

A Variety of Responses, Mostly by North Americans

Bennett, John C. *The Radical Imperative: From Theology to Social Ethics.* The Westminster Press, 1975.

The best single volume in which to observe white, male, North American responses to black theology, feminist theology, and Latin-American theology.

Berger, Peter. *Pyramids of Sacrifice: Political Ethics and Social Change.* Basic Books, Inc., 1974.

A critique of assumptions that either "growth" or "revolution" can be easily adopted as models of social change.

Bigo, Pierre. *The Church and Third World Revolution.* Orbis Books, 1977.

A careful and cautious treatment, showing interrelationship of readings from history, the gospel, Marx, and the future.

Conway, J. A. *Marx and Jesus: Liberation Theology in Latin America.* Carlton Press, Inc., 1973.

A survey of contemporary positions, with special attention to Alves, Assmann, Comblin, Gutiérrez, and Segundo.

Fierro, Alfredo. *The Militant Gospel: A Critical Introduction to Political Theologies.* Orbis Books, 1977.

A militant book, criticizing "political theologies" from the basis of a radical "historico-materialist theology."

Herzog, Frederick. *Liberation Theology.* The Seabury Press, Inc., 1972.

A pioneer attempt by one of the first white theologians to deal with liberation themes in response to black theology.

Holland, Joe. *The American Journey.* Center of Concern, Washington, and IDOC/North America, New York, 1976.

A reassessment of U.S. history and experience, showing how familiar events look when seen from the standpoint of the poor and oppressed.

Houtart, François, and Rousseau, André. *The Church and Revolution.* Orbis Books, 1971.

Includes chapters on Cuba and Latin America.

Lehmann, Paul Louis. *The Transfiguration of Politics.* Harper & Row, Publishers, Inc., 1975.

A treatment of revolution, confrontation, transformation, and politics in a Biblical context that also draws on Marx, Mao, Castro, Torres, and the Black Panthers.

McFadden, Thomas (ed.). *Liberation, Revolution and Freedom: Theological Perspectives.* The Seabury Press, Inc., 1975.

See particularly Fiorenza's comparison of European and Latin-American theologies, and Shaull's account of his theological movement since returning from Brazil.

Napier, B. Davie. *Word of God, Word of Earth.* United Church Press, 1976.

An exegetical study of the Elijah stories illustrating an interplay with liberation themes.

Neal, Marie Augusta. *A Socio-Theology of Letting Go: The Role of a First World Church Facing Third World Peoples.* Paulist Press, 1977.

Sketches the need for a theology of diminishment, relinquishment, and "letting go," as the appropriate response of the nonpoor to liberation theology.

Reist, Benjamin A. *Theology in Red, White, and Black.* The Westminster Press, 1975.

Responses to black theology and Native American theology that go beyond white guilt toward a triad of mutual interdependence.

Ruether, Rosemary Radford. *Liberation Theology.* Paulist Press, 1973.

Essays responding to Latin-American concerns in a North American context, from a feminist perspective.

Torres, Sergio, and Fabella, Virginia (eds). *The Emergent Gospel: Theology from the Underside of History.* Orbis Books, 1978.

Papers from a conference of Third World theologians at Dar es Salaam. An important work by the ablest exponents of "the view from below."

Torres, Sergio, and Eagleson, John (eds). *Theology in the Americas.* Orbis Books, 1976.

Deals with the question, What do *we* do with the concerns raised by liberation theology? Includes papers and discussion from the "Theology in the Americas" conference in Detroit in 1975.

Wagner, C. Peter. *Latin American Theology: Radical or Evangelical?* Wm. B. Eerdmans Publishing Co., 1970.

A strong critique of liberation theologians, from an "evangelical" perspective. Helpful bibliography.

Winter, Derek. *Hope in Captivity: The Prophetic Church in Latin America.* London: The Epworth Press, 1977.

Interviews with church leaders along with examples of liberation theology in action. A readable account for the nonspecialist.

LITERATURE IN SPANISH

Literature in English on liberation theology is but the tip of the Spanish iceberg. Many important books are not yet translated, a few of which are listed here:

Alvarez, Alfonso (ed.). *Fe Cristiana y Cambio Social en America Latina.* Salamanca, 1973.

Papers from a gathering of Latin-American theologians, including Gutiérrez, Scannone, Comblin, Assmann, and others.

Araya, Victorio. *Fe Cristiana y Marxismo: Una Perspectiva Latinoamericana.* San José: Litografía Lehmann, 1974.

A volatile work describing various levels of the presence of Marxism in reflection and faith, and a treatment of the implications for Christians.

Castro, Emilio, *et al. De la Iglesia y la Sociedad.* Montevideo: Tierra Nueva, n.d.

Papers by members of ISAL (Iglesia y Sociedad en America Latina), including Alves, Niilus, Castillo, Arce, Shaull, and others. Good bibliography.

Cussianovich, Alejandro. *Desde los Pobres de la Tierra: Perspectivas de Vida Religiosa.* Lima: C.E.P., 1975.

Plea by a Salesian priest for radical identification with the poor as the hallmark of the religious life.

Dussel, Enrique D. *Historia de la Iglesia en America Latina.* Barcelona, 1974.

A historical study, revised several times to keep it up to date.

Gheerbrandt, Alain. *La Iglesia Rebelde de America Latina.* Mexico City: Editorial Siglo XXI, 1970.

Documents and interpretive comments about the Medellín conference in 1968.

Gutiérrez, Gustavo. *Teología Desde el Reverso de la Historia* Lima: C.E.P 1977.

A historical essay indicating differences between the "dominant theology" of Europe and North America and the "liberation theology" of Latin America.

Liberación: Diálogos en el CELAM. Bogotá: Secretariado General del CELAM, 1974.

Pro and con essays sponsored by the Latin American Bishops Conference (CELAM). More con than pro, illustrating attempts to draw away from the implications of liberation theology.

Maldonado, Enrique, *et al. Liberación y Cautiverio.* Mexico, 1976.

Papers from a large Latin-American conference on theology, held in Mexico City in August 1975.

Oliveros, Roberto. *Liberación y Teología: Genesis y Crecimiento de una Reflexión, 1966–1976.* Lima: C.E.P., 1977.

A major work, assessing all the important individuals and movements of the last decade.

Richard, Pablo. *Cristianos por el Socialismo: Historia y Documentación.* Salamanca: Sigueme, 1976.

Augments the materials available in Eagleson (ed.), *Christians and Social ism.*

Scannone, Juan Carlos. *Teología de la Liberación y Praxis Popular.* Salamanca: Sigueme, 1976.

Essays written between 1972 and 1974, dealing with the contribution of popular cultural movements.

Signos de Liberación. Lima: C.E.P., 1973.

Documents from the whole of Latin America, dealing with liberation themes. A useful sequel to *Signos de Renovación* (available in English as *Between Honesty and Hope*).

DOCUMENTATION AND PAMPHLET MATERIAL

IDOC/ North America, 145 E. 49th Street, New York, N.Y. 10027.

Provides extensive documentation of global movements, with excellent resources for Latin-American liberation themes.

Jesuit Project for Third World Awareness, 5430 South University, Chicago, Ill. 60615.

Mimeographed translations of current Third World theological writings from a variety of sources.

The LADOC "Keyhole" Series, United States Catholic Conference, Box 6066, Washington, D.C. 20005.

Pamphlets containing primary source materials. Typical topics: Paulo Freire, Social-Activist Priests, Latin Americans Discuss Marxism-Socialism, Women in Latin America, The Theology of Liberation, and other topics.

Latinamerica Press, Apartado 5594, Lima 1, Peru.

Weekly eight-page news bulletin with excellent coverage of the church in Central and South America.

NACLA (North American Congress on Latin America), Box 57, Cathedral Station, New York, N.Y. 10025, or Box 226, Berkeley, Calif. 94701.

Provides documentation on the economic relationship of North and South America, with frequent materials on the Latin-American church.

"Options for Struggle: Three Documents of Christians for Socialism," published by CRIPS, Box 223, Cathedral Station, New York, N.Y. 10025.

Reports of Conferences in Santiago, Ávila, and Bologna that state a Socialist Christian perspective. CRIPS also provides other documentation material.

Radical Religion: A Quarterly Journal of Christian Opinion, Box 9164, Berkeley, Calif. 94709.

A publication of the Radical Religion Collective, emphasizing liberation themes, Christianity and Marxism, reading the Bible from class perspectives, etc.

Indexes

Index of Names

Index of Scripture Passages